ARE YOU COMING QUIETLY?

Tales of a Kidsgrove Bobby in the 1960s.

by

Trevor Houlton

CHURNET VALLEY BOOKS

Published by
CHURNET VALLEY BOOKS
43 BATH STREET
LEEK
STAFFS ST13 6JQ

ISBN 1 897949 18 9

Printed in Great Britain by the Ipswich Book Company, Suffolk

CONTENTS

Photographs by the author
Illustrations by Nicola Richardson

HOUSE TO HOUSE COLLECTION

One unusual aspect of police training, is the two year probationary period served by all officers, during which your services can be dispensed with at any time! In other words, if you do not reach the standard they want, they can sack you without much explanation.

I was constantly reminded of my three predecessors at Kidsgrove who were dealt with in this manner. One poor chap who had previously been a bus conductor, was discovered to be unable to control school children when it was his turn to supervise them crossing the road. With this threat at the back of my mind I launched myself into every situation with enthusiasm and determination wherever offences seemed at all possible. Unfortunately, this enthusiasm was often my undoing, as my lack of background knowledge of the local population combined with even less knowledge of my senior officers, meant that my zeal required considerable fine tuning.

Yellow lines had just been introduced and the local florist seemed immune to these new restrictions. The problem was proving that the brightly painted van used by the florist was being left on the yellow lines for reasons other than loading or unloading. I did not like losing a court case, therefore I wanted to build up good evidence of this flagrant disregard of the rules. After spending a great deal of time observing the vehicle's comings and goings, my evidence seemed firm enough to confront the offender - during a six hour period the vehicle had only left the no waiting area for half an hour! Quite clearly, a good funeral order had kept the florist busy in her basement.

My approach to the shop was full of confidence; no need to rush after six hours of observation! I had rehearsed the lines over and over in my head. I opened the shop door, causing a bell to ring in the basement. Within seconds we were face to face. I had expected some sign of panic at the sight of my uniform, followed by words of apology but she seemed to remain completely unperturbed.

"Is it your van outside, madam?"

A silly question really, as it was obvious to both of us that it would be highly unlikely for the butcher to own a van with the words 'Say it with flowers' written all over the side.

"Yes it's mine," she replied, "is anything wrong?"

I explained that it had been parked on yellow lines for five and a half hours and unless it had broken down, this was an offence. Driving licence and insurance were duly inspected before I left the shop saying, "the full facts will be reported".

Just half an hour of the day remained for me to write the offence book up ready for court and yet another successful day would bring me nearer to the end of my probation. Well not quite! I handed the book into the Inspector who read it from cover to cover. I was sure no mistakes had been made and I waited for his praise.

"You will never learn, will you lad?" the Inspector said as he tore the book into small pieces and threw it onto the fire. What on earth had prompted this reaction I thought; but somehow it did not seem the right time to ask for an explanation. Later I was taken to one side by the Sergeant.

"You haven't been here long enough to know everyone in the town or the rules about who is who. Some of the people out there help us a lot and deserve a break now and again."

It was many weeks later before I was able to finally unravel the reason for my downfall. The answer was quite simple; every week the Inspector collected a bunch of flowers from the florist and took them home to his wife. My use of the word 'collected' should not, of course, be substituted by the word 'bought'.

With this brush with the Inspector fresh in your mind, it will not come as a surprise to discover that within 18 months of my arrival at Kidsgrove I moved; but it was not as a punishment, far from it; I was now to take on the responsibility of a one-man police station at Talke Pits, some four miles from Kidsgrove but still under their command. It was unheard of for anyone with under 20 years service to be given such responsibility, but for someone still on probation; surely they must be Chief Constable material, I thought!

The village was a busy place, as far as police work was concerned, comprising terraced houses and pre-war council houses, an oil factory, a large scrapyard and a private coal mine with its hard-working, hard-drinking men. The police station was now a part of my home and I was as a result, available 24 hours a day, seven days a week. One Sunday evening, I was relaxing watching a rather blurred picture on the black and white secondhand television - it amused visitors when the picture vanished from the screen and I was to be seen in the garden twisting the aerial around a pole tied to the garage. I certainly couldn't afford an aerial on the chimney of the police station, considering the high cost of its removal if we moved again. A knock came at the front door and I opened it to see a well-dressed man accompanied by a small child and a terrier dog on a lead.

"Can I help you?" I asked, half expecting him to ask if my father was in; members of the public were often confused by the sight of a 20 year old policeman running the village police station - and a pair of jeans and a T-shirt were the normal off-duty garments worn by this local officer.

"Yes; I am making the annual collection from the village to give the old folks a party at Christmas," he said.

My eyes scanned the assembled group in front of me and memories flooded back of the law regarding such collections. What faced me was a perfect exam question, full of offences against the laws designed to prevent fraud or intimidation. No dog should be present and certainly young children should not accompany a collector - and where were his badge and sealed collection tin? More especially, had this collection been authorised by way of a permit from the Chief Constable? I certainly had not received any notification!

While trying to get to grips with the full circumstances, I searched my pockets in an effort to find some coins to throw into his bucket.

He said, "I am Councillor Jones and this collection has been made annually for over a hundred years. We always collect from the police station - no one has ever mentioned needing a licence from the Chief Constable before. I can assure you, it's all above board and for a good cause, officer."

Not wishing to appear totally mean, I threw some coins into the bucket and told him to report to Kidsgrove Police Station at 9am on Monday morning; but the collection must stop and matters would be sorted out by the Inspector then! I went back to the television feeling rather smug to think that no one had even thought to ask if the Council had ever applied for a licence to make the collection. The fact that it had continued unlawfully for a hundred years must surely score some extra house points for me. I even patted myself on the back for not charging Councillor Jones on the spot, thus giving the Inspector no opportunity to criticise me for jumping the gun! Every angle had been covered; I thought my actions were beyond reproach.

The following day, I was on the early shift, helping out with a vehicle check by the Ministry men. My brief explanation to the

Sergeant at Kidsgrove, that I had uncovered an illegal house to house collection the day before, was met with a certain amount of amused derision.

"If he turns up, we will deal with it. You go and sort the vehicle check out, lad - the men will be waiting for you." It was pointless to enter into an argument and I left the station muttering to myself that the Councillor would not be amused when he discovered that I was miles away on a vehicle check. Sure enough, the Austin patrol car arrived at the vehicle check at 9.15am with a desperate-looking Sergeant at the wheel.

"The boss wants you urgently. What the hell have you been up to this time?" he growled.

I walked up the station steps and entered the main office. The Councillor was sitting in the small waiting room with a cup of tea in his hand. He smiled at me but I had no idea whether this meant he was in trouble or I was. The Inspector's door opened and I could see immediately from his red face that whatever he thought about the situation, I was not in his good books. The door slammed shut behind me and I stood looking at his typist who was perched on a chair ready to take notes. He said in an unusually restrained voice, so that the Councillor in the next room could not overhear, "Do you know who that is? You couldn't have brought a more dangerous man into this station. What are you saying he has done?" I quickly outlined the facts to the Inspector who was clearly out of his depth. Law books covered his desk, all open at pages referring to street collections and lotteries.

"You show me where it says you need a licence." His agitation calmed a little when he realised that my knowledge matched the wording in the law books.

"Right Rona," he said to the typist, "take a letter from Councillor Jones to the Chief Constable. 'I wish to apply for a licence on behalf of Kidsgrove Council, to make a house to house collection.........'." He was certainly going out of his way to help Councillor Jones, I thought, but when the letter was finished and had been signed by Councillor Jones, he even stuck a stamp on it! I was ushered out of the office while pleasantries were still being exchanged and the Sergeant told me to get back to the vehicle check. It was clear that I was most unlikely to be offered a ride back in the police patrol car and so I made my way to the front door. Suddenly, Councillor Jones was alongside me and to my astonishment, he struck up a conversation.

"I'm glad that you pointed out the law to me young man. Why no one told us about it before beats me. Fancy the Council breaking the law every year and collecting from the Police Station into the bargain. It's good to have someone like you around the village. A fresh face can do wonders to reduce crime. Where are you going now?" I explained that a vehicle check awaited me some miles away and without hesitation he said " I'll take you there in my car, its the least I can do after dragging you back like this."

We walked down the station steps side by side and I looked back wondering what the reaction would be if I took up his kind offer. The faces of the Inspector and Sergeant could be seen watching the Councillor's departure. What the hell, I thought; why shouldn't I get in his car. He seemed to be one of the few people on my side at this moment in time and he could prove a useful contact in the future. As I climbed into the front seat and placed my helmet on the floor, I glanced back towards the station windows; both officers were transfixed at the sight of me in the car and I tried hard not to smile. I can only guess what words were exchanged as Councillor Jones drove me off to the vehicle check!

YES I DO TAKE SUGAR

Sudden deaths are one aspect of police duties which can be unpleasant. It took me some time to come to terms with the fact that someone who had lived on this earth for over 85 years, could possibly be described as having died suddenly! Surely someone of that age has had a good innings and nothing could be more natural than turning your toes up!

The Coroner certainly did not see it that way and each one was treated as being suspicious until the contrary was proved. The doctor was usually the first one to be called and if the poor old patient had not been visited by him during the previous two weeks, making the cause of death difficult to determine, the police would be summoned to investigate. I felt that it did not require a genius to work out the cause in most cases - the gas cooker was popular for suicide in those days and a head in the oven resting on a pillow would certainly have resulted in an immediate call for my assistance, you would have thought! The process always went along similar lines and one morning I was sent along to a small terraced house where a man in his 80's had died in bed. As we get older, our eyesight fails and hygiene standards slip through no fault of the individual. I became something of an expert at gauging if it was safe to drink the cup of tea offered me or whether to partake in a slice of homemade cake. All police officers have entered the kitchen where any resting of papers on a flat surface will result in them sticking as securely as ready-pasted wallpaper. They will also have experienced the three piece suite which looks inviting but whose webbing beneath the cushions is about as strong as the elastic in a pair of well-worn Y-fronts! Down you go into the jaws of the settee, unable to release yourself without the use of mountaineers' ropes and pitons!

From the outside of the terraced house, I was able to get an indication of what the inside would reveal. Paint was peeling from the window frames and you could write your name in the dirt on the glass. The widow of the recently deceased came to the door and invited me in – she had been informed by the doctor that I would be along shortly after he left. It was rather dark inside and the smell of mothballs drowned other fragrances.

"I'm sorry that I have to come round but I'm afraid this has to be done if the doctor cannot issue a death certificate, my dear," I explained.

"It's no trouble," she said, filling the kettle from a tap screwed to the wall, "would you like a cup of tea?"

The place had not enlivened my taste buds and a quick look around the room confirmed my fears that even malaria might dwell in the loaf of bread lying on the table. "No thank you, I have just had a cup of tea at the station, my dear. I will spend the rest of the day in the toilet if I have any more; thanks for the offer though," I replied, hoping that she would not take offence. Having sorted out the problem of the tea, I decided to get down to the real job in hand.

"Where is your husband?" I enquired.

"Upstairs in bed," the old lady replied, "Go on up."

I climbed the stairs and entered the bedroom. He was dead alright and neatly covered with the bedclothes, as if asleep. My next move was to roll him over to ensure the there were no visible injuries which might cause questions to be asked later. It does seem commonsense to check for this type of thing but a high ranking colleague of mine once fell foul of this elementary proceedure. He attended a woman who had collapsed at her home and on arrival summoned the services of an ambulance. Her husband described how she tripped and fell while using a carving knife to cut a joint of beef. She was loaded into the ambulance and her distraught husband was requested to accompany her to the hospital in the back, which he agreed to do. Only on arrival was it discovered that the poor lady had several quite seperate stab wounds in her back and the husband was promptly arrested for attempted murder!

My old gentleman was quite free of any such suspicious injury and I wrote out a label to identify him and attached it to his big toe. Returning downstairs, I began to take a full statement from his wife which had to include all aspects of his health from the day she met him. Shrapnel wounds from the war and short spells in hospital were all included, culminating in an account of his last few hours of life. He had woken at 7am and spoke of feeling unwell and his dutiful wife had asked if he felt like eating any breakfast. A decision was reached that he might manage a soft boiled egg and some thinly cut bread 'soldiers'. At this stage in the statement, she announced that a cup of tea was brewing in the pot and I found it difficult to refuse her offer, having been in the house for over an hour by this time. The story continued with the old man sitting up in bed eating his boiled egg until suddenly he let out a gasp and died suddenly.

"Do you take sugar?" she asked, as I completed the statement.

"Yes please, one spoonful," I conceded, not wishing to cause offence. My eyes were by now quite accustomed to the darkness of the room and what I saw next filled me with horror. She placed a spoonful of sugar in my cup and stirred the tea. As the teaspoon was withdrawn from the cup I could see quite clearly a large piece of egg yolk on the spoon - it was certainly the very same egg which had been the last meal eaten by the old man and now some of it was in my tea. You might ask the question - did you throw the tea away? The answer is NO - I drank it thinking of England!

POLICE DOGS ARE SO USEFUL

The village had its fair share of characters and was certainly not short of people willing to make a few dishonest pounds if the chance arose. Although only 20 years old, I was well used to the ways of the world by now and within a very short time had a mental list of those not to be trusted.

George Pointon, who lived next door to the village pub, was one such character. He always had a motley collection of old cars and vans parked at various angles in his front garden. George was in his 30's with two young children and he didn't see why he should waste his hard earned money buying tax discs for his vehicles when they ran perfectly well without them!

His failure also, to pay the rates bill on his house, resulted in the issue of many distress warrants which instructed me to mark up goods in his house for sale, but we soon came to an understanding where I would push a note through his door following which he would call at the police station within a few days with the outstanding amount. In those days George used this system rather like we use credit cards nowadays.

We also played a cat and mouse game when he used his vehicles, involving me watching for movements of the cars and George working out when I would be off duty. Although in principle I could report him for offences at any time, I always felt that it was a little underhand when I was not on duty! His favourite game was to use a car which he had bought and was taxed by the previous owner, and to continue to use it for the 14 days grace allowed after the tax ran out. There was little point in reporting the driver during this period as he only needed to go to the Post Office and buy a disc from the start of the month and no action could be taken. If during those two weeks grace at the start of the month he could avoid being seen on the road, he would leave the vehicle off the road for the next two weeks and only re-tax the car from the start of the next month. He would therefore get two weeks use free of tax.

My way of dealing with this much used system, was to

make a note in my pocket book of all cars seen on the road with expired licences during this two weeks of grace. I then waited until a new licence was applied for and requested a copy of the application form. You may recall that one question on the form asks, 'If the date from which the new licence is to start is not consecutive with the expiry date of the old licence, has the vehicle been used on a road during this time?' Bingo! George fell for it time after time. Not only was he prosecuted for having no tax disc during the missing month, but also for making a false declaration to obtain the licence.

Another of the systems used to avoid paying for a tax disc, was to cut out a section of another disc (usually stolen) and stick the part with the date of expiry over your own disc. What most forgot, or didn't realise, was that the date of expiry is also printed in code at the top of the disc. The serial number always started with the month of expiry, ie, 1 26593472 meant it expired in January. Likewise, 7 64390442 meant it expired in July.

George must have been really fed up with me at times because when I first arrived in the village he was still a learner driver, on top of all his other problems. As I stood in the entrance to the Co-operative shop doorway one day, minding my own business, along came George in one of his newly acquired vehicles. Although he was on my side of the road, he was already too close for me to stop him safely and as I moved to the edge of the footpath he ducked down behind the steering wheel in an attempt to hide his face. At Court, he entered a 'Not guilty' plea to driving whilst unsupervised and without 'L' plates and I was required to give evidence.

"Yes, your Worships, I am sure it was George Pointon driving the car and as it went past me I shouted, 'It's no good hiding Georgie; I can see it's you.'" The Magistrates were as convinced as I was and it was a move George never tried again.

George lived some 100 yds from Queen Street which housed a motley collection of people, ranging from an eccentric man with a Polish name, whose house was almost full of old newspapers, to local villains who were difficult to catch. Although there were only isolated cases of cars being stolen in the village itself, the local CID were most put out by an upsurge of cars being stolen in Tunstall and abandoned in Talke Pits. The matter became so serious that the Detective Sergeant at Kidsgrove himself became involved, no doubt at the request of his opposite number at Tunstall whose crime figures were going through the roof!

The Detective Sergeant was unorthodox to say the least but he certainly seemed to know all the local criminals and what they were up to. He once took me to a number of houses in the village to make a search for stolen property. It was clear that my uniformed presence was designed to make things look official since he never considered obtaining search warrants, seeing paperwork as something which never achieved results. On our visit to various homes the system was always the same, a knock on the back door followed by his right foot taking the lock completely off the door frame. "Must tell the Council about security, these locks are useless," he would say as the frame could be heard to splinter and the lock fell to the floor. It was some time before I realised that it was highly unlikely for anyone to be in any of the houses anyway, as the occupants had already been locked in a cell for several hours before the search started.

The whole station had now become involved in the attempt to stem the flow of 'borrowed cars' which vanished in Tunstall only to be found abandoned in Talke Pits. Maps appeared in the CID office with green pins marking the street from which the car had vanished and a blue pin showing where each one was found. It became a matter of routine when a car was stolen fron Tunstall, for a search to be made in the Queen Street area of Talke Pits. Sure enough the vehicle would be parked, undamaged and insecure, with nothing having been stolen from inside it.

Crime conferences were organised and observations kept but all to no avail. Two routes were recognised which might be taken by the culprit and our Austin patrol car spent most of Friday and Saturday evenings parked on one or other of the routes. The Detective Sergeant had narrowed the field down in his own mind and two names had come to the fore as contenders for the crimes. Matters had now reached a critical stage which involved the Newcastle dog handler being drafted in to help. I had seen the dogs in action at football matches in Stoke and although they were very effective at clearing rowdy youths, the dogs also often 'nibbled' police officers legs! It has always puzzled me why they seemed unable to differentiate between a man in a uniform wearing a large hat and someone in a T-shirt and jeans. Perhaps their eyesight is not of the same standard as their sense of smell!

Observations on the possible routes had proved fruitless and it was decided to concentrate all efforts on the Queen Street area. It had passed through my mind that if we did not keep asking the owners to collect their cars after they had been abandoned in the street, then the locals would not be able to park their own cars in the street! By this stage both uniformed officers and the CID as well as the dog handler were spending hours pacing the streets in the village and the Detective Sergeant was desperate to nail the culprit. "He's got to be caught this weekend whatever happens," he growled, just before the group of us dispersed on observations. He really means business, I thought; God help the felon when he gets his hands on him - valuable CID drinking time was being lost on this little episode and tempers were wearing thin!

It was pitch black as we set out down the High Street and after about an hour the Detective Sergeant greeted me with the good news of a telephone call to the station. "A red Cortina's been taken from Tunstall in the last half an hour; have you seen the dog handler?" he enquired. We walked together along the rows of terraced houses and by good fortune met the dog handler. Only minutes passed before we discovered the Cortina, engine still warm, not far from Queen Street. This was the break we had been waiting for. Now all that was needed was a good track from the dog. His tracking harness, a leather affair which went both around his neck and between his legs, was put on and down went his nose onto the pavement beside the Cortina. There was no rain to spoil the track and I was excited at the prospect of a good chase. Police dogs follow the smell of recently disturbed vegetation, not as some people think by first sniffing an item of clothing. The only time this method is used is when an item such as a handbag or body needs finding - the dog can differentiate between natural surroundings and a handbag, discarded for instance in a field. The track being followed on this occasion was caused by small stones being disturbed when the culprits feet trod on the pavement; on a summer evening we can smell a freshly mown lawn - a dog can detect the same smell from a few blades of grass which have been crushed beneath your feet.

Off we all set behind the handler, with the dog picking his

way carefully at a slow walking pace. But, within a few minutes, the dog had lost interest and found a few doggy sniffs around a lamp post. "He's normally so good at tracking," said the somewhat embarassed handler, trying desperately to cajole the dog back to his task, but I could tell that the Detective Sergeant was not amused. The track had gone in the general direction of Queen Street until it had petered out, which seemed to convince him that his suspicions about the culprit were correct.

"Get hold of the dog and follow me," he said, and none of us dared to ask what he had in mind. Not a word was said as we walked along past the front doors of the houses in Queen Street.

"I'll do the talking, you just keep quiet," he said as we approached the front door of one of the houses. The downstairs light was on, which was a good sign as most of the occupants of neighbouring houses were now in bed. He banged on the door with his fist and I dreaded to think what would have happened if no one had answered it. But after a few moments the door opened about 18 inches and the figure of a man stood looking round the door. The Detective Sergeant pushed the door open to reveal a man of about 25 years of age wearing a suit. Even to my somewhat untrained eye, he seemed just the type we were looking for and his dress showed he had been out for the evening to the bright lights of the City.

'What's up," he said, glancing between the dog and my uniform. I looked at the Detective Sergeant, wondering what sort of wisdom would come from his lips now and I didn't have to wait long.

"Bill James; you're under arrest for stealing a car."

"What do you mean; what car?" came the reply.

"A red Cortina taken from Tunstall tonight. The police dog has followed a track from the car right to your door."

"Bloody hell, I never thought I'd get caught by a bloody police dog; just let me get my coat," he said. The Detective Sergeant followed him into the house and I could hear the beans being spilled about some of the other cars he had taken. I looked at the dog handler and he stared at me. "What chances that man takes; he's just played a hunch on this one and he's hit the jackpot!" I said. The dog handler just nodded back to me, no doubt embarassed that he could not really claim the glory for his dog.

In order to achieve detection rates well in excess of 50%, this type of police work was an every day necessity! To be fair, I don't think that innocent people were ever convicted, but I am sure many more guilty ones appeared before the Courts.

FIND MY GNOMES, OFFICER

The Chief Constable was Arthur Morgan Rees, a man keen on rugby and who always showed a great affection for the officers under his command. His driver would flash the headlights of his white Jaguar whenever the Chief approached a foot patrol officer, in order to warn him of their approach and the Chief Constable would wave back at the saluting Constable.

An illustration of the Chief Constable's caring attitude was when I was a part of a contingent of officers at Uttoxeter racecourse. I was standing in a narrow country lane directing traffic towards the entrance gates on a particularly hot afternoon. Our uniform was not designed to be comfortable in hot weather and rules laid down over many years forbade the rolling up of sleeves or the removal of ties!

A narrow track led up to a large imposing house overlooking the racecourse and I became aware of the voice of an elderly lady who had appeared from behind a stone pillar at the entrance to the driveway. She beckoned me towards her and pointed to a tray which she had placed on top of the stone pillar. On the tray was a pot of tea, several china cups and a plate full of cream biscuits. She indicated that the tea was for the police officers on traffic duty and promptly walked back up the driveway to her home.

The Chief Constable was expected to arrive at the racecourse within the next ten minutes and the officers within shouting distance of me indicated that they would love to quench their thirst with the freshly brewed tea, but what would happen if the Chief Constable arrived early and caught us holding cups and saucers in our hands, when we should have been waving our arms at the traffic? Although each one of us desperately wanted a drink, none of us was brave enough to leave our duty point to pour a cup, fearing a charge of neglect of duty.

The Chief Constable eventually arrived, waving to each one of us as his car glided by on its way to the main enclosure. The tea was by now too cold to drink and we were all too busy with the volume of traffic to think of the kind gesture by the old lady. It would have been kinder to throw the tea into the hedge, but we were all too preoccupied with duties around the racecourse.

The following day the Inspector received a telephone call from Headquarters regarding the incident. The old lady had telephoned the Chief Constable to express her indignation that we had not touched the tea, so lovingly provided. Far from doing the right thing by remaining on our traffic points, we were told in no uncertain terms that on any future occasion we must drink the tea. The Chief Constable wished it to be known that he expected us not only to drink the tea but also have a chat with the old lady if she started up a conversation. He was not concerned that we might be missing from our traffic points for a few minutes or that we might not be able to salute him properly with a cup in our hand.

This willingness to deal personally with relatively minor matters was again in evidence when a letter arrived on his desk complaining that Kidsgrove Police had taken little action to stop the theft of garden gnomes from a front garden. In today's climate, such letters would merely be stamped at Headquarters and forwarded to the relevant station for further attention. But this letter was acknowledged in person by the Chief Constable. It was then forwarded to to our Inspector together with instructions that positive action was required and that, as well, a reply outlining the outcome was to be returned within three weeks.

Being a town centre foot patrol, the responsibility for tracking down the culprits lay squarely on my shoulders. The CID were to assist by mounting observations on the tiny front garden which, despite the thefts, still appeared crammed with every type of gnome immaginable! The practice on the night shift was to leave the station at around 10.10pm and check all shop doors for security within the first hour of patrol. When this was completed each officer could then patrol his allotted area as he pleased, unless required to attend an 'observation point', usually a telephone box where he could be contacted by the station. After 11pm most people had deserted the town centre and any noise could be heard from a great distance in the silence of the night.

The dark uniform gave almost invisible protection if you stood in shop doorways, which was a ploy used in the same way that video cameras now operate.

I had been in a doorway for about 10 minutes one night, watching and listening when I heard in the distance the sound of a large group of youths walking towards me from the direction of the Town Hall. I was near to a zebra crossing at the bottom of a steep hill on the main road through the town. Not wishing to be noticed I moved back into the doorway as far as possible and listened to the boisterous noises getting closer. Gradually they came into sight beneath the street lights to my left and one of the group jumped up in an effort to strike the globe of the belisha beacon. It would have been easy to move out into the light and cough loudly to attract their attention, which would have resulted in them moving off quietly, but this was not my style. I remained motionless in the doorway and watched for developments!

It was always a risky business because without communication my only hope of rescue, if set upon by such a large group was to blow my whistle. What I had been hoping for then happened; two of the group lifted another member into the air next to the belisha beacon on my side of the road. I could see that the light inside the globe was not flashing but that its partner on the other side of the road was working correctly; this did not seem of any significance to me at the time. Within seconds, the youth had removed the large globe from its mounting and had thrown it into the gutter, none the worse for its ordeal. Should I make my move now and arrest them for a breach of the peace or wait to see what they did next? I decided to remain still for a few minutes longer as I was quite invisible to them and I still had a bird's eye view of what they were doing.

The one youth was still perched above the other two, near to the now beaconless pole and with his outstretched hand, he reached out for the bulb. A quick twist and it was in his hand as his comrades lowered him to the ground. This was far better than a simple breach of the peace, now it had developed into a full blown larceny! Now was the time to make my move; quickly and with a certain amount of stealth I came out of the shadows - thank goodness for rubber-soled shoes, no metal tips on my heels to give advanced warning of my movements. Within a few paces I was able to take hold of the arm now holding the light bulb.

"You are under arrest," I said. My thoughts were totally committed to dealing with the offender but I was soon surrounded by a throng of arguing youths who demanded that I let him go.

"He's done nothing," "Let him go," came the demands of the group. The youths surged around me but I took a firm grip of my prisoner's arm and started to drag him bodily down the footpath towards the police station. It was only 150 yards away but I needed all of my strength of purpose to stick to the task, determined that despite the efforts of his comrades, I would eventually reach the steps of the station. A great deal of pushing and shoving took place but the group failed to act in unison, which quite possibly would have secured his freedom.

With a certain amount of relief, I climbed the steps to the station and burst into the charge room. The noise had disturbed the Sergeant from his game of snooker and he demanded to know what the gang of youths were doing outside. I breathlessly explained how they had tried to stop me arresting the prisoner and without a further word, he opened the station door and herded them all inside. A hurried conversation then took place between the Sergeant and the station constable, following which chairs were placed in one of the rooms to form a large circle. All of the youths were told to sit down and silence settled over them within seconds. The Sergeant's words took me by surprise.

"I want to know who has taken the gnomes and you are all staying here until I get an answer," he boomed. I was still trying to gather my thoughts concerning the light bulb and the gnomes were the last thing on my mind; however, things quickly started to fall into place. The youths had walked from Tunstall right past the garden which was causing us so much grief. Could it be true that these were the culprits? Scarcely had my mind begun to ponder the probability of rescuing the station from the wrath of Headquarters, when the silence of the youths gave the game away. Silence was a certain indication of their guilt in our minds, yet insufficient to ensure a conviction of course.

The next move by the Sergeant was textbook stuff. It was

highly unlikely that any one of them would own up to the offence and be seen to let the others down. What was needed was the opportunity for them to discuss the matter in private, thus reaching a group decision.

"I will give you five minutes to think about it before I lock you all up," said the Sergeant, and we all left the room to give them some thinking time; in those days claims of unlawful arrest were laughed off by experienced officers and prisoners could languish in a cell for days without the fear of a solicitor banging on the door with a fist full of papers to serve on the police. The ploy worked perfectly. When we re-entered the room, they all admitted being involved in taking the gnomes as a practical joke. The police car was brought out from the yard and driven to a field where the missing treasures were found safe and well beneath a large hedge.

The delight on the Inspector's face the next morning was clear for all to see as he dictated a report outlining the capture of the gnome stealers. The letter of complaint was firmly attached to the report and placed in the night post bag in order to be on the

Chief Constable's desk the following day.

His problem may have been over, but mine was only just starting as I went through the definition of theft. The stolen light bulb was causing me a certain amount of anxiety in that on close inspection it had a broken filament which rendered it useless for its purpose - it had not been flashing because it did not work - in order to steal something it must have a value, even if this is only a penny, but what value would you put on a burnt-out bulb?! The bulb in question was no ordinary household bulb for which a replacement could be obtained from Woolworths. No, this bulb had a unique screw fitting all of its own. I thought long and hard before deciding to visit the local Council Depot and to this day I cannot recall what expanation I gave for wanting a bulb to fit a belisha beacon, but I returned triumphant.

Six weeks later, I attended the Magistrates Court clutching my newly aquired light bulb with an exhibit label duly attached. To my dismay, no one asked to see the evidence let alone check to see if it worked! Never mind; the yobs had got their just reward in the form of a stiff fine and the subsequent press story ensured that future possible vandals would think twice before causing mayhem in our town.

IT'S JUST A PARCEL

In the late 1960's a scrap metal yard existed on the outskirts of the village between the A500 and the A34. It occupied a triangle of land with small country lanes on two sides and was piled high with an assortment of cars well past their sell-by date. The owner's house stood at the point of the triangle where the two lanes met. To say the least, the business was not popular with the local Council who on more than one occasion had applied to have it closed, siting vermin as one of its reasons. Word had it that many years ago the business had started on a small scale which was tolerated by the authorities until it grew to its present size. The main problem for the Council was proving that the business was relatively new and therefore subject to a planning application.

For my part it was extremely useful to have ready access to cheap parts for my Ford Popular, which being a 1954 model was always in need of repair. The owner, John Frost, would remove the parts for me himself rather than allow me to spend time searching the yard for a particular item. This was not an act of kindness towards the local Constabulary but ensured that I was out of the premises quickly and saw as little as possible! When on duty, I would make frequent visits to check his books in which were recorded the names and addresses of all customers selling metal to him. The system was introduced to trace people who 'found' metal items some of which had vanished from church roofs in mysterious circumstances. Man-hole covers were a very popular thing to be weighed in at back street scrap yards and as long as an entry had been made in the book, the scrapman was in the clear. Occasionally, stolen metal could be traced from the register but anyone who thought they could find the thief from the name given in the register were usually living in 'cloud cuckoo land'! Some names were quite amusing and showed criminals have a keen sense of humour. Apart from the numerous John Smiths, there were the Mr A Field, Caravan Park, Dudley or Mr ARD Luck, Trent and Mersey Canal Basin. Any police officer will tell you that only the man from Littlewoods Pools receives any help from itinerants when trying to locate one of their fraternity; if you happen to be in uniform, the doors of the caravans do open - just to let the dogs out for a run round!

Although I was the village police man, any enquiry of significance was retained in the CID department for internal consumption only. A strict line was drawn on a 'need to know basis' which was why I was kept in the dark about observations being carried out in the village by a squad from Headquarters CID. I later learned from a local shopkeeper that he had noticed a group of strangers in a car hanging about the village. In those days it was generally accepted that most crimes took place under cover of darkness and the squad had spent many sleepless nights lying low around the scrapyard. Indeed the offence of burglary in the daytime was the lesser offence of housebreaking which caused the police to lose many cases when clever solicitors argued that their client had entered the building shortly before sunset and not shortly after. The CID squad would no doubt be entering the village before closing time in order to take some liquid refreshment, thus making the night pass a little quicker!

One day each month, I was required to attend Newcastle Police Station to join as many other officers as possible to discuss crime trends and exchange information. These meetings lasted well into the afternoon and I was always one of the first to escape back into the fresh air. The drive back in my old Ford Popular gave me time to digest the information discussed at the meeting. One innovation had just arrived and I was now in possession of it - a small hand-held radio which gave me instant access to my fellow officers at Kidsgrove Police Station. As with all new technology, some people were able to learn its intricacies relatively quickly while others like the Inspector were heard bellowing into the mouthpiece, "hello, hello", completely unaware that to receive a reply the transmission button must be released!

I drove past the scrapyard on my left, intending to turn right at the give way sign at the junction. My view to the left was partly obscured by a bright yellow articulated lorry in British

Railways livery. This type of vehicle was a common sight in the area and deliveries were made to shops in the village. The lorry had a large tarpaulin sheet covering the load on a flat bed open trailer. As I made the right turn something told me things were not quite right; call it intuition or just a policeman's devious mind but it caused me to slow down and look in my rear view mirror at the lorry. It was as if I was seeing something for the second time and my mind started working overtime. It all came flooding back; not a week previously I had seen a similar lorry in exactly the same position, right outside the house owned by Frost. It was decision time. What if Frost was one of those lucky individuals who regularly received deliveries by British Railways; he would not take too kindly to a nosy young policeman questioning him about a simple delivery. My day had been long and I was due to finish duty in a few minutes anyway. I was about to drive off when the driver of the lorry walked from Frost's front door back to his vehicle and climbed onto the trailer. What harm would I cause by just asking a few questions, I thought, as I walked the thirty yards towards him. Frost was nowhere to be seen and I engaged the driver in conversation.

"All right mate; you seem busy; I saw you here last week didn't I?"

"Yes," he replied quite calmly, "I do all this area." But my next question was not answered in quite such a confident manner.

"What have you delivered?"

"A couple of parcels," he replied, securing the cover on the load.

"Can I have a look at what you have got on the back?" I said. The driver now became quite agitated.

"Why; what's the problem?"

"Oh I just like to know what's going on in the village and I'm curious to know what John Frost is having delivered," I replied. His next move came as quite a shock but it had exactly the opposite effect on me to that which he intended.

"I'm a special sergeant in the police at Newcastle and I don't like your attitude," he said angrily. At that moment John Frost appeared from his front door and said to me.

"What's the problem youth?" He always addressed me in this way, which should not be taken as indicating disrespect; the word 'youth' in this context is a friendly greeting in Stoke on Trent.

"I just wondered what you've had delivered John?" I replied.

"A parcel of baby clothes; the wife has just had a baby," came his answer.

"Can I see the parcel, John?" I said.

Whether it was a slip of the tongue by the driver when he referred to delivering a 'couple' of parcels I couldn't be sure, but matters were getting extremely suspicious in my eyes. After about three minutes Frost emerged carrying a cardboard box about one foot square, loosely tied with string, which was handed to me. This co-operation shown by Frost was most disconcerting and my suspicions that I had stumbled upon something were getting stronger. The parcel was opened revealing various items of baby clothes in plastic bags and on the outside of the box was a label bearing Frost's address. I was determined not to let the two men fluster me but for some unknown reason Frost returned to his house leaving me holding the parcel.

"I thought you told me it was a couple of parcels?" I asked the driver.

"I was mistaken, can I go now, I've got a lot more deliveries to make. If I am late, I'm going to complain about you," he said reaching into his wallet and showing me his police officer's warrant card.

The label on the parcel had attracted my attention and added to my suspicion. The writing was in block capitals and rather scruffy with the name of the village wrongly spelt. Talke Pits was spelt Talke Pitts - which would later prove to be vital evidence. I was sure that the men were hiding something but what else could I do? The only other thing I could think of was to look at the rest of the load on the lorry.

"Can I see the load please?" I enquired.

"No, you have no power to look and I'm leaving to make my deliveries," he said. This was not the reaction I expected from a fellow officer, whether he was a regular officer or a part-time special. What would the Detective Sergeant do in such circumstances, I thought to myself. He would not just accept the situation and walk away! I had no idea if I had the power to look at the load but my mind was made up. Without saying another word I pulled the edge of the tarpaulin sheet nearest to me upwards while the enraged driver tried to hold it down. For a few minutes, the two of us engaged in a tug of war straight out of a Laurel and Hardy film. Finally, I won the day exposing at least half of the load which consisted of cookers and fridges mixed with parcels of various shapes and sizes. Labels were attached to each item showing their intended destination, but none were anywhere near Talke Pits!

The driver stood motionless waiting for my next move. My gaze was suddenly taken by four green boxes right in the middle of the load, almost hidden by larger boxes placed around then. They were unlike the other boxes in that they were metal with carrying handles on each side. A closer inspection showed that they were destined for Radway Green, a Royal Ordnance factory just over the border in Cheshire. I had no idea what they contained but it seemed strange to use British Railways to deliver locked metal boxes.

"You have seen the load; now can I go?" said the driver in exasperation.

"I'll just see if the CID can pop along and have a look," I replied.

The driver walked towards the cab of the lorry forcing me to take his ignition keys. I walked towards my car, out of earshot, leaving the driver tying the sheet over his load; now was the time to use my new fangled radio.

"PC Houlton to control; over."

"Receiving, go ahead."

"Any chance someone from the CID can meet me at Frost's scrapyard, soon? I don't know what's going on, but I'm being given the run around by Frost."

"Sorry, they are still not back from the meeting at Newcastle."

"I can't hold things much longer, I need them fast, you know how crafty Frost is. Send them as soon as they get in.

Over and out."

At least I wouldn't be on my own much longer and a problem shared is a problem halved, I thought. What was it that the driver and Frost were trying to hide? The parcel was still firmly gripped under my left arm and the lorry ignition keys were in my pocket. What more could I do until the CID arrived? I took up a position on the footpath where the two lanes met, which ensured that I could see both the front and back of the cottage together with the lorry. If Frost wanted to dispose of anything he had had plenty of time to do it, but there seemed little more I could do.

From my vantage point, I saw an old car parked in the lane near to the back entrance to the scrapyard. To my horror it suddenly pulled away and came towards me. Instinctively, my right hand was raised as I stepped into the path of the car which stopped a few yards in front of me. If the driver was attempting to remove anything from the yard I was determined to find it. The driver was most co-operative allowing me to remove every item from the vehicle including the rear seat.

All of the items, from tools to pieces of carpet were piled up on the footpath as my search for anything unusual went on. The driver accepted my explanation for the search and luckily was the type who was solidly behind the police. This was fortunate because the search revealed nothing and it was with some embarassment that I helped him return the car to its previous tidy state. The radio suddenly crackled into life.

"It's the DS speaking, Trevor. What's the problem?"

"I don't really know, Sarge; I could be onto something good or else I am in deep trouble. A British Railways lorry has delivered to Frosts and the driver is a special sergeant who tells me I am going to be reported for delaying him."

"Don't let him go! We are on our way."

At least, I had told someone and if I was in trouble, the DS was the type to stand by me. What I didn't know, but the DS did, were the facts concerning the observations being carried out by the heavies from Headquarters. Within minutes the CID arrived and I quickly told the DS of my encounter with both Frost and the lorry driver. He always spoke very quickly, rather like machine gun fire and he thought at the same speed.

"Yes, Yes," he answered each time I showed him a piece of evidence. He then gave me clear instructions.

"Take the driver back to Kidsgrove. You get in the passenger seat of the lorry and wait at the station until I get there." The driver turned the lorry around and we had travelled about half a mile when the radio came into life again.

"Come straight back with the lorry," came the order from the DS. As we drew up outside the front door of Frost's cottage, no explanation was needed. The door was lying flat on the floor in the hallway of the cottage. I knew at once that the DS had used his powers of persuasion, mainly with his right foot, to gain entry. Alongside the door was a pyramid of green metal boxes identical to those still on the lorry. It soon became apparent that I had stumbled upon an outwardly lawful method of delivering stolen property, but what was in those boxes?

I helped load about twenty boxes onto the lorry and saw that Frost was now firmly handcuffed to one of the CID officers. We all returned to Kidsgrove Police Station in convoy where I was introduced to some high ranking army officers who arrived shortly after us. The boxes were opened to reveal large quantities of ammunition. I had never seen so many bullets in my life. The Detective Sergeant took me to one side and congratulated me.

"This is the best arrest we have had for years. I shouldn't be surprised if you get a commendation for this little lot," he said - but I didn't! I watched as phone lines became red hot, with calls being made to British Rail executives and the Army stores depot. More CID arrived and then left again in groups. The first headed for the Army depot which resulted in more arrests. The second group visited the home of the special sergeant, returning with stories of an Aladdin's cave of stolen electrical goods. It transpired that all deliveries were placed on a long concrete loading bay allowing drivers to back up their lorry and take whatever items were on their round. It was easy for them to select goods from another pile and spirit them away. No items were ever signed for and loads were never checked! A day later, the special sergeant was willing to tell everything, for which he received a shorter sentence from the Magistrates, on the understanding that he would be a prosecution witness against Frost. It was quite unusual for prisoners to engage a lawyer but Frost had money, enabling him to hire the services of a good barrister - his story then became quite plausible:

"I run a scrap metal business and one day a man came into the yard offering to sell some surplus ammunition. Naturally I was concerned that the items might be stolen but when he showed me his police warrant card and I saw that he was driving a British Railways lorry, I was convinced that it was all above board. Buying from a policeman seemed a safe thing to do and I bought several loads from him in order to melt down for scrap."

Within a few months Frost appeared at the Quarter Sessions (now the Crown Court) for trial and his story was eloquently put to the jury by his barrister. I gave my evidence which culminated in the production of the parcel Frost had handed to me. Frost entered the witness box to give his evidence and was then questioned by the prosecution barrister.

"We have all heard your version of events Mr Frost. Do you agree that you tried to convince the constable that what had been delivered was a parcel of baby clothes, thus hiding the fact that boxes of bullets had been delivered?"

Frost answered, "I just panicked really. The constable has a certain reputation for poking his nose into things and I knew if I told him about the boxes he wouldn't believe me."

"Can you write down for me your name and address on this piece of paper please?" the barrister added. Scrap merchants have never been renowned for their spelling ability and Frost was no exception. He produced his name and address using block capitals, which showed a remarkable resemblance to the writing on the parcel.

"I see that you spell Talke Pits with two T's in 'Pitts', exactly the same as the address label on the exhibit. Frost looked down and nodded his head. The realisation was just dawning on him that despite all the efforts of his lawyers, the evidence against him was looking overwhelming.

"You wrote that label in order to put the constable off the scent, didn't you Mr Frost?" Frost's face looked resigned. He had taken the gamble of a jury finding him not guilty but instead of a short term in prison at the hands of the magistrates, he could now face a much stiffer penalty.

The jury returned a guilty verdict and the Judge was not impressed by the fight Frost had put up in an effort to gain his freedom. "For this serious offence, which could have had far reaching implications due to the nature of the stolen goods, I sentence you to eighteen months in prison," he announced.

Frost glared at me and said, "I'll have you for this when I get out." I said nothing, but thought how vulnerable I was in such an isolated police station! Within weeks, Frost's family moved out of the cottage back to Wales where other relatives were on hand to help. The scrapyard was closed and the land cleared by the Council who uttered a grateful sigh of relief. So much time had gone into their efforts to close the yard but in the end, a policeman's chance intuition had got the job done for them.

Frost's threats fortunately proved to be unfounded and now, many years later, I haven't seen or heard of him since that date.

THE PROBLEM WITH ANIMALS

Most police officers in those days had previously held other employment before joining the force, bringing with them untold skills in different fields. In most stations you could find a joiner, a bricklayer or even a fireman from a steam locomotive - I never came across a train driver - no doubt it was not thought fitting to revert to being a lowly paid policeman after being a highly skilled - and paid - driver of a steam locomotive.

Because I joined the police at a young age as a cadet, my only experience was from a year spent selling shoes in an old fashioned shoe shop, where the linoleum was polished weekly and the brass fittings daily. But my one special skill, learnt from the tender age of 12 years, was pigeon racing. I had been given two birds of excellent pedigree and had spent a great deal of time training and racing them. Pigeon racing was very popular in North Staffordshire and it soon became my way of getting to know the locals.

While at Talke Pits, I rescued a pigeon which was lying in the road when I was on traffic duty and the bird was found a home on the flat roof of the police station. The bird was found a mate and lived in a large wooden box above the rear entrance. Word quickly spread amongst my colleagues that when problems were encountered with animals, I was the one to be called! One Sunday morning, I entered the foyer of Kidsgrove Police Station to collect my paperwork when I was greeted by the station constable.

"Just the man," he said, "some children brought a seagull in last night. It has got a broken wing, so we put it in the CID garage. Can you have a look at it before I call the RSPCA?"

It was good to feel that my expertise was proving useful and I opened the garage doors to look for the unfortunate bird. We had only recently moved to the new station and the CID van was parked neatly inside, blocking my view of the floor. I scrawled along the side of the van and reaching the back, I saw the seagull standing in the far corner, just visible in the darkness. Handling a racing pigeon is a simple affair requiring only one hand around the birds wings, whilst securing its legs between two fingers. You may have seen seagulls from a distance but I can assure you that when viewed from close quarters, they are the size of a chicken! I approached with caution, not wishing to lose him through the open garage doors, creating further problems for myself. He did not move from the corner as I gently placed both hands around his body, making sure that the damaged wing would not be further injured.

I emerged from the garage triumphant, with the intention of displaying my skills to the station constable and anyone else who happened to be around. Entering the foyer, my confidence grew and I took hold of one wing in order to fan it out and check the bird's injury. Apart from the actual size of the bird, I began to appreciate the nature and size of its feet and beak. Its feet were like large oak tree leaves and its beak was several inches long and viciously curved. As I examined the bird, so he began examining me; having spent the night in a dark garage, he was only now adjusting to the bright lights of the station and beginning to be able to assess his captor. Just as the station constable walked towards me, the bird decided to take action. Its head turned to one side and in a split second, the beautifully sharp beak dug into my right forearm with the power of a pair of pliers being squeezed by Geoff Capes! Despite wearing a long sleeved shirt and tunic, the pain was unbearable. The more I shook the bird to make him let go, the more he thrust his head into my arm. He had managed to get a half inch piece of my flesh in his beak and the more I fought, the more pressure he exerted.

"Open the door quick," I shouted to the station constable and I ran towards the front entrance. Broken wing or not, the ungrateful bird was about to be thrown bodily into the street. My throwing action was like that of a rugby player as the seagull became involuntary airborne, but he did not flutter to the ground as I expected. No, he soared into the sky as gracefully as any other seagull, without the slightest hint of injury, let alone a broken wing. I returned to the station and removed my jacket in order to check my condition. Although the skin was not broken the area was badly bruised. I could hear the station constable recalling graphic details of my recent encounter to the various nearby stations as I left. News such as this travelled fast!

My next encounter with with a bird came on a rainswept morning on the waste land near the village of Talke Pits. A small lake with an island in the centre was the main feature of about ten acres of scrub grassland. Nearby a filthy stream with high embankments flowed down to a river. I was walking alongside the stream when I noticed a beautiful white swan floundering in the stream, seemingly unable to fly, its feathers soaking up the water instead of repelling it. My first instinct was to descend the embankment and pull the unfortunate bird out; however my recent reward for helping the seagull was a reminder to stay well clear until I had worked out a good plan.

It was raining hard and my thick gaberdine raincoat was even heavier than normal and water was seeping down my neck, soaking my shirt collar. Some will recall the old shirts with no collar attached, which required two studs to hold the collar in place; the general idea was that a clean shirt would last two days with a change of collar each morning. Some took advantage of this by only changing the shirt every four days, by which time even a blind person would be aware of their approach at a 100 yards down wind! One stud held the collar at the front, directly in line with your adam's apple, whilst a shorter stud held the back of the collar in place. After wearing the collar for a good eight hours, the long stud at the front had made a dent in your neck like a tracheotomy hole!

For about ten minutes I stood watching the swan and its battle for survival, flapping its wings occasionally in an effort to mount the embankment but only suceeding in pulling its body a little clear of the water before falling back into the stream again. It was like watching a survival programme on television, when a young animal is being stalked by a lion and you know that very soon it will be dead - if you could only intervene!

I paced up and down the embankment looking for a place where the swan could extricate itself from the filthy slurry but it was a man-made embankment and uniform in height throughout its length. Even when I approached the swan, its fear of me did

not give it the power it needed to drag itself up the opposite bank. Soon he was extremely tired and he stopped even trying.

As a child I had been warned that a blow from a swan's wing could break a man's arm and although this particular swan was not very fit, I did not want to take any chances. I would need surprise and speed to reduce the chance of any retaliation by the bird. Despite a search for something to throw over the swan to engulf its wings, the only thing I could find suitable for the purpose was my raincoat and in view of the heavy rain, I was not prepared to part with it. I pulled out the chin strap of my helmet and placed it firmly under my chin to avoid it being dislodged in what I felt would soon turn out to be some wrestling match!

The bird seemed more subdued than ever as I stalked it. I kept perfectly quiet and approached it slowly so as not to lose my footing on the wet grass of the embankment. The swan had its head down and its wings at its side, as I came to within a few feet and stood motionless to allow him to get used to my presence. He had obviously managed to find a raised part of the bed of the stream to stand on, as he was clearly not using his feet to paddle. We stayed in our positions for what seemed a long time, watching one another intently - but it must only have been a few minutes. Suddenly I made my move, diving with my arms to cover his wings, hoping that he did not decide to peck my face. Thankfully, his wings were easy to hold together as I lifted him from the water even though my leather gloves were now rather squelchy inside. I pulled his body to my chest, placed my right arm round the bird and held his neck in my left hand. Climbing the embankment again was no easy matter and I slipped and slid, falling to my knees in the mud on more than one occasion.

At last I reached level ground and made a cursory examination of the bird. I had a warm feeling inside as I approached the edge of the lake which lay still and quiet except for the myriad rings of the falling rain. The swan was quite plump near his breast and I felt sure that within a few hours he would be back to his old self and swimming gracefully round the lake. I lowered him into the water with the care of a proud owner of a new model boat he had spent the last twelve months fixing the sails of! The swan started to paddle in the fresh water and to my delight was soon 30 yards out into deep water. He seemed quite pleased and he ruffled his feathers and occasionally stretched his wings.

Although I was by now wet and cold, I felt it was a success story, which I would be able to recall to myself with warm satisfaction on those long foot patrols in the middle of winter. But not quite! As I started to walk away, I could see more of the lake including a part previously hidden by the island. My friend was not going to be lonely, I thought, when I caught sight of two more swans gliding towards him. I envisaged a grand reunion of the three birds, but I quickly realised that this was not to be; the two new swans, clearly a male and a smaller female, caught sight of my friend and headed straight for him. He suddenly started to paddle frantically in the opposite direction, but despite his efforts to get clear of the pair, they had soon overhauled him.

Both swans pecked his neck and to describe their actions as hostile would be an understatement. Quite clearly they were not going to allow him to remain on the lake despite the fact that it seemed large enough to accommodate a dozen or more swans. With increasing ferocity the two birds attacked my swan, pushing his head below the water and holding it there. He escaped a number of times only to be cornered again. I was unable to help him. Only a boat would let me get near to him and boating was not a pass time enjoyed by people of Talke Pits in those days! Reluctantly I returned to the station where I decided to telephone a friend in the RSPCA. I told him the whole story and was not prepared for his explanation.

"He probably went into the stream to get away from the other swans. When adult swans pair off, they will not accept another swan anywhere near them during breeding. He probably won't survive if he can't fly from the lake," said my friend.

The words stuck in my mind until the next day when I was able to go back to the lake to see what had happened. To my horror, my RSPCA friend was right; the two mated swans were swimming graciously around the lake with their heads held high and my bird lay on a mud flat near to the island, quite dead, his neck outstretched in the mud. The two birds had pushed his head into the mud and drowned him - what an end for a magnificent bird - and caused by his own kind! Nature can be so cruel.

THE FRIENDLY GOOSE

On my arrival at Kidsgrove Police Station in 1966, I was introduced to the various staff, ranging from the typist to the cleaner but I was not prepared for what lurked in the backyard. At some stage the garden at the rear of the station had consisted of lawns and fruit trees, but volunteers were few and far between when it came to cutting the grass! The solution had been to acquire a large white goose which served two purposes; the first to keep the grass under control, and the second, to keep trespassers out of the garden. He was a fearless creature who would advance upon anyone or anything that entered the garden, flapping his wings and running at a great pace, his beak wide open and his neck outstretched. If you ran away, all was well, but if you stood your ground and confronted him, you would receive a severe peck on the leg, followed by many more until you left.

Roaring coal fires were a feature of the station, being as it was in a mining area where coal was plentiful. The heat given off made you so warm and cosy that it took a great effort to return to patrol after enjoying a meal break in mid-shift. A long leather chaise-longe stood next to the firegrate in the mess room, a long narrow room with doors at both ends. There was a large dining table with thick oak legs placed beneath the window and allowed seating for about ten people. Chairs to relax in - a motley collection salvaged from salerooms - were spread around the far end of the room. One door led to the much used snooker room and from there into the rear yard, whilst the door at the opposite end gave access to the control room with its telephones and filing cabinets, not to mention another roaring coal fire!

The chaise-longue was the regular resting place for the night office constable taking an unscheduled nap when things were quiet - and this could quite easily develop into a deep sleep. One morning at around 4am, I returned to the station to be met by a ghostly silence except for the constant ringing of the large black telephone in the control room. I found the night office constable, Arthur, sound asleep on the chaise-longe and it took me some time to rouse him. It would have been easy for me to answer the telephone myself but it would not be good protocol, especially as the call would no doubt be from our parent station in Newcastle; the public did not usually bother us at that unearthly hour in those days. I shook Arthur gently and gradually his eyes blinked into life, staring into space for a few seconds and revealing a pink colour where the white of his eyes should have been. He shook his head in a further effort to bring himself round and rose to his feet.

"OK, OK," he said and after a short pause, continued, "I just dozed off for a second." He made his way towards the telephone and lifted the receiver, "Kidsgrove Police," he said, followed by a long silence as the person on the other end flooded his ear with what I took to be a sharp telling off for being kept waiting so long.

Arthur was not one to be "caught napping", if you will pardon the pun, and his razor sharp mind went into top gear immediately. "I am well aware that the phone has been ringing for a long time, Sir, but we don't have the advantage of gas heating here and I was out in the backyard collecting coal for the fires." Arthur was certainly not acting defensively. The "Sir" in his reply meant only one thing to me - it was the Inspector from Newcastle on the other end, and he was not amused at being kept waiting. Arthur's next move proved a real stunner. Having explained the fictitious reason for the delay, he continued to put the icing on the cake!

"Yes Sir, I can take the message now but you will have to wait a few minutes or ring me back. My hands are filthy dirty from the coal and I will have to wash them before I can write anything down." The authority in Arthur's voice was really impressive and by now the tone of the Inspector had changed to one almost of apology. Arthur placed the receiver on the table and walked towards me, showing me his clean hands and winking. Without a word he turned on the tap and allowed the water to cascade into the large ceramic sink, making as much noise as possible. He turned the tap off, waited for a few moments and took hold of the telephone handset once more.

"That's better Sir; now I'm in business; what was the

message?"

When the call was completed, Arthur stared at me with a look of experience and said,

"Thanks for coming in when you did, son; the Inspector said he was sorry to have snapped at me and appreciates how busy the station constable is at night with all these extra tasks to perform. It will take a better man than him to catch me out!"

The nights were long and during meal breaks we would often put the world to rights, with deep discussions on wide-ranging topics. When we had finished our meal, the scraps of food left over were thrown to the goose. I say thrown advisedly, because it would be a brave and foolish person who tried to hand feed the goose - it remained aggressive at all times.

The oldest station constable was Ken Lord, too old to patrol the streets but the ideal person to deal with enquiries received at the desk. Being the youngest and often most controversial constable, I would be teased by Ken over many matters. In particular, he would often rag me and say I was afraid of the goose; which was perfectly true - everyone was afraid of it. But matters came to a head one night when my shift coincided with his and I was unable to take the ribbing any more. I finished my sandwiches and on the pretext of giving the goose some crusts, made my way out through the snooker room into the yard. It was pitch black and I was wary of the goose seeing me before I saw him, in which case I would have to retreat very quickly!

The goose used an old dog kennel for shelter and I gingerly looked inside with my torch. Sure enough the startled bird had been asleep inside the kennel but the beam had woken him. In an instant the torch went off, leaving him once again in darkness and allowing me to grope inside the kennel with my gloved hands. The bird was in no position to attack me in the dark as I put my hands around his body and took a firm grip of his wings. He remained quiet apart from kicking his legs as I lifted him close to my body.

Triumphant, I entered the snooker room with the bird under my arm and went straight to the control room where I knew Ken would be. Things would have been fine if I had kept the goose in my grasp, but I decided to show off!

"Afraid of the goose, eh? Not me, Mr Lord," I said, bending down and releasing the bird onto the polished linoleum. The look of outrage on Constable Lord's face would have been sufficient reward but I knew it would have the bonus of finishing off, once and for all, his constant remarks about me being afraid of the bird.

"Get it out of here," Ken demanded, but any thought of me returning the bird to its kennel evaporated when it took to flight. The bright lights in the station meant he could now see everyone and he made the decision to flee rather than attack us. Within seconds, with wings flapping wildly, the goose had run along the floor to within a few feet of the open fire.

Matters now became seriously out of hand, as officers from various upstairs rooms descended to see what all the commotion was about, only to be greeted by an agitated bird flapping about wildly in an attempt to take off. My main concern was preventing the bird singeing his wings as he flapped past the roaring coals but all he succeeded in doing was causing some of the burning coals to fall onto the linoleum. His wildly beating wings caused a rush of air so strong that the coals fell up to a distance of two feet onto the highly polished floor. The plight of the bird was forgotten as the station shovel was found to scoop up the burning embers. But no matter how quickly they were picked up, burn marks became evident on the linoleum!

By this stage there were four or five of us attempting to corner the terrified bird who had made good use of the open doors in the station to repeat the performance with the fire in the mess room. It would be fair to describe the scene as 'all hell let loose', as the goose was shooed into the snooker room where the lights were quickly extinguished. It was clearly my responsibility to recapture the bird and my guilty conscience overcame my fear. Safely grasped under my arm, I returned the unfortunate creature to the yard, pushing him back into the dog kennel.

Not a word was spoken as I left the office to continue my night shift; enough damage had been caused for one night! The one satisfying outcome was that I silenced beyond doubt, the taunts of those who said I was afraid of the goose. I also wondered to myself whether it would make the bird have a healthier respect for someone in uniform in future but the answer to this question was soon found to be "no" and a stick had to be provided by the back door for use of anyone daring to venture to the dustbin!

SICK AS A PARROT

Although I was not at Newcastle Station when the incident occurred, the following true story refers to a mythical bird and shows how police officers with a wicked sense of humour can cause serious consequences. The CID worked from one large office which had it's advantages in that conversations could be overheard by colleagues. This allowed information to be spread through the team without the need to call constant meetings. Casual remarks and overheard telephone conversations were remembered by those not directly involved in the case, which could then be useful when answering questions in the middle of the night. It is much more reassuring for a member of the public to hear; "Oh, yes I am sure some of your property was found yesterday in a raid on a house," than; "I am sorry but the officer dealing with your case is not on duty and I am unable to help you." It gives the impression that the whole station is aware of Mrs Smith's burglary, rather than just the officer who attended.

But this sharing of knowledge is an acquired art which must only be used with great discretion and on certain occasions - it is not a blank authorisation to go telling the whole world the workings of the station. Some overheard conversations can be quite damaging, especially if the information is meant for personal consumption only, such as personal and domestic problems. Unfortunately some individuals who have ears the size of elephant's, coupled with a strong desire to gain brownie points with senior officers, seem adept at gathering all this gossip. It had come to the point when even the slightest whiff of scandal would find its way to the top - when that was the last place anyone with any sense or decency wanted it to go.

Several snippets of information had thus found their way into the wrong hands, where a great deal of damage had been done to the individuals involved. In the end, things became too serious to let rest and a decision was taken to find the culprit and silence him for good. By carefully allowing certain individuals to overhear information, it was soon easy to trace the source of the leaks. Then with great skill, a plan and course of action was decided upon. The need was not only to plug the leak, but also to let others know that it was not a good career move to upset the applecart by bleating to the management!

A few days later, a small group of CID officers could be seen gathered in a clandestine fashion in the corner of the office, running their fingers down the fine print of the 'For Sale' advertisements in the local paper. There it was for all to see, tucked away in the livestock section: **Free to good home. African Grey Parrot, complete with cage. Good talker – repeats everything it hears.**

The paper was quickly replaced in the general office tray. The telephone number given was none other of course than that of the CID officer involved in the leaks. It was not long before the advertisement started to produce results, which was perfectly understandable, given that a talking parrot was, and still is something of great value. The telephone rang at regular intervals for two whole days destroying the peace and tranquility of his rest days. When he could stand it no longer, his telephone number was changed!

Although it seemed hilarious to the whole station and the force beyond, the reaction of senior officers seemed slightly over the top. A full scale disciplinary enquiry was instigated by Headquarters resulting in everyone being interviewed at length. But as usual in such circumstances, the enquiry ground to a halt when everyone expressed complete surprise at such a stupid prank and denied all knowledge of it. The saying used in the force at the time and still just as relevant today is, "If you can't stand a joke, you shouldn't have joined!"

MY FIRST POSTING - KIDSGROVE

After my 13 week intensive course at the Police Training Centre at Ryton-on-Dunsmore near Coventry, I was ready to be let loose on the general public - but were they ready for me? One by one, my classmates and I entered the office of the Assistant Chief Constable to be told where we were to be posted. The look of shock on my face when the word Kidsgrove was announced produced the question, "Do you know where Kidsgrove is?" "No, Sir," came my reply. He advised me to get a map out - and this only confirmed my suspicions that the town of Kidsgrove was as far north in Staffordshire as anyone could be posted to, without ending up in Cheshire!

My trusty Ford Popular carried me to the main A50 where I was told the police station was located. It was a Saturday and Stoke City were playing at home and a double decker bus had pulled up right outside the station. I parked behind the bus in time to see Arthur, a stern looking constable with a boxer's nose, alight from the bus. He had a jaunty look about him, having apparently just warned the football fans that any kind of unruly behaviour would result in a visit to the cells!

Arthur was an old fashioned bobby who stood for no nonsense. Some time later I saw the way he dealt with an unreasonable neighbour of his, who insisted on mowing his lawns on Sunday mornings when Arthur was in bed following his night shifts. The following week, when Arthur completed his night duties, he announced to everyone that he was not going to bed as usual at 6am, and his words as he left the station were, "Let's see how they like the sound of a motor mower when they are in bed." Arthur went home and by 6.15am was thrashing his motor mower up and down his lawn! His neighbours obviously got the message as we never again heard that Arthur's beauty sleep had been disturbed!

The police station was a large old house with steep steps made of blue engineering bricks leading up to the front door. When the steps had been climbed, it could be seen that there were two small lawns in front of the station and these lawns were destined to receive a great deal of my attention when the time came for station fatigues. An impending visit from Headquarters would be preceeded by instructions to cut the grass and scrape moss from between the blue bricks both on the steps and around the station. The Inspector assured me that he would provide the tools from his own home to do the job - I don't know what I expected but I was certainly surprised when he produced an old kitchen knife to remove the moss and a tiny pair of shears to cut the grass. I spent many an hour on my hands and knees making things spick and span in time for the arrival of the senior officers!

Although, when I first arrived, we did not have any kind of transport, it was not many months before a grey Austin Cambridge arrived. It was a standard model straight from the makers, apart from a tiny metal sign saying 'POLICE', which had been screwed to the front chrome grille. The screws holding it in place were never allowed to go rusty as the CID often removed the sign for undercover work! No car park existed for police use and the Austin languished in the locked yard of the Co-operative

Undertakers when not being used by the station sergeant - but I did get to see it when it needed a polish!

When you entered through the main front door of the station, the heat from the coal fires could be felt, and the smell of the polish on the highly shined linoleum added a homely fragrance. I was to become quite used to the smell of polish, as I applied vast quantities of it to the floor on quiet Sunday mornings. An inventory, listing every single item from a desk to the telephone, hung in an oak frame as each room was entered. The inventory was signed by the Superintendent and provided an instant check if anything was missing.

Ken Lord was the recognised station constable for the daytime and he wrote everything in a beautiful copperplate handwriting. He had been there so long that I sometimes fully expected him to be listed on the inventory along with the tables and chairs! A long leather bench stood against the wall in the mess room and a very popular snooker table took up most of another room. I could not play the game but there were many experts - no doubt the result of the many hours of practice. Ray Reardon was once a Stoke bobby and no doubt his great skills were honed to perfection during the long hours of night duties. Indeed it was difficult to find any police station at that time without a snooker table.

All of the station books were written up by Ken Lord. Every telephone call and visitor to the station was recorded in one of the large beautifully bound books. Often, the same message would be repeated in several of the books and despite my wish to see the system streamlined, the tried and tested method was not be changed; but I did have one small victory concerning what we called the Red Books, issued to every officer on joining. The purpose of this book was to record every item of money received and then to forward both the Red Book and the money to Newcastle, where the money was counted, the Red Book stamped and duly returned as proof that it had been received. The system seemed to me to be very slow and certainly not foolproof. I asked PC Lord what happened if during its journey the money vanished. It seemed that this had never happened and therefore was not an issue for discussion.

But I seized the opportunity to raise the matter during one of the many inspections made by Headquarters.

"I can't understand why we have Red Books, Sir," I said to the Inspecting Officer. The look of disgust from my own Inspector said it all; how dare this young upstart question the use of a system which had been tried and tested for years? The senior officer certainly didn't appreciate my Inspector's attitude and said to him, "Let him speak, Frank; we need some fresh ideas. I am sure there is a good answer to his problem." I was pleased that my voice was being listened to for once and I explained that when I received some cash for a shotgun licence, I completed a receipt for the applicant, took his money and entered full details of it in the Red Book. I then sent the whole lot to Newcastle and waited for several days before receiving it back. In the mean time, I might have collected money for rates (even then people only paid at the last minute when I arrived with the summons) and I would be stuck with large quantities of money until the book returned. I also questioned what happened if the money vanished in transit. The outcome was that, within a few weeks, all the Red Books were collected in and never used again. There were no bonus schemes in those days for bright ideas and it has never been mentioned from that day to this. No doubt the senior officer claimed the credit for saving a great deal of time and effort!

I soon settled into a routine and Kidsgrove became my home for several years - a busy place for a young officer to learn the many tricks of the trade.

HANGING AROUND BATH POOL

Bath Pool was and still is a very picturesque place, where people go for country walks around the large lake just a few minutes drive from the city of Stoke on Trent. It earned notoriety shortly after I left Kidsgrove around 1970, when Leslie Whittall was found hanging in an underground passage near to the lake. A pathway leads walkers right around the lake and there are areas of woodland which rise up steeply from the edge of the water.

I had often parked my car at the edge of the lake and walked my dog around the various pathways. It was an autumn morning when one such walker out with his dog in the woods, rang the station to say he had found a body. I listened to the radio messages but did not get involved myself because it was not within my area of patrol. Only when I had pieced together the full details of what was happening did I make the decision to go and have a look myself; my inquisitive nature and my enthusiasm to learn all I could, forced me to poke my nose into what was fast developing into a major enquiry for a town the size of Kidsgrove. The truth is many police officers never get the chance to visit such scenes - so I took my chances whenever they presented themselves.

The body had not been found lying on the ground but hanging in a tree. By the time I arrived, much of the preparatory enquiries and actions had been put into motion and the scene was a hive of activity. The photographer arrived from Headquarters at the same time as I did and I helped him carry his equipment from the car park to the scene. The wood was about 40 yards wide on ground which rose from the lakeside pathway to the summit. I am not very accurate with elevations but the hillside was certainly quite steep, sufficient to make standing in one place without spreading your feet wide very difficult.

I had always been intrigued as to how the police could be sure that someone had hung themselves as opposed to someone else having hung them against their will and then making it look like suicide. This case would be a really valuable piece of learning, I thought to myself, and I was eager to absorb every scrap of information that came my way. The leaves had fallen from the trees leaving the trees bare and I could see a small group of CID and uniformed officers gathered around the body, which was swinging about in the breeze. The body was that of a man clothed in a jumper, trousers and overcoat. The ligature appeared to be a dog lead tied to the thick branch of a tree some nine feet from the ground.

The officers gathered around the Inspector to discuss the various theories gleaned from the scene so far. The conclusion was that it was quite possible that the man had climbed the tree on his own, put the ligature around his neck and fastened the other end to the branch - you might say that it was as easy as falling off a log! In order to convince the assembled group of this theory, one officer scrambled up the tree and went along the branch for a short distance before climbing slowly down again. By now, the camera man had assembled his tripod, with a certain amount of difficulty because of the terrain. The camera was eventually positioned level with the tree and he spoke to the Inspector before retiring behind his camera and waiting for the wind to turn the body to face the camera. I was intrigued by the activity of the CID officers, who struggled to assist the cameraman by taking hold of the body's wellingtons and moving him round to face the camera. Unfortunately, as soon as they released the boots to move out of camera shot, the man slowly swung around again to present a back view. I was unsure why it was imperative to obtain a photograph of the corpse face on, especially as his tongue was protruding some three inches out of his mouth - not at all a pretty sight!

This manoeuvring seemed to go on for several minutes and it produced a certain amount of hilarity among the assembled officers. I have no doubt that you might probably by now be thinking along the same lines as I was on that day - has a doctor been to confirm officially what we already knew? I had not seen one and I decided to ask the Inspector a simple question which at the time appeared to me perfectly natural, but seemed to hit him like an exocet missile.

"When we did first aid at the training centre, we were told to check for a pulse and then for signs of breathing. As it is obvious that he is dead, sir, do we leave bodies in the position we find them until the doctor arrives or do we cut them down? If we ever thought that they might still be alive, would we cut them down immediately?"

I could see the brain cells suddenly working overtime in the Inspector's head and he was clearly confused. He looked towards the photographer, who by this stage had managed to obtain some good face view shots. Without answering my questions, he signalled to the photographer to come to him.

"There has been a change of plan. Destroy the film you have taken. We are going to cut him down and then you can take the photographs."

Quite clearly my intervention, although not intended, had caused a rapid change in tactics. As I stood watching, the senior CID men huddled together in conversation with the Inspector. It soon became apparent that the body was to be cut down from the tree; a three man operation which involved me - I had now changed from being a passive onlooker to being a part of the enquiry team. In order to prevent any further injury to the body which would surely happen if the ligature was just cut allowing it to fall to the ground, it was decided that two men would take hold of the legs to give support first. I took one leg and another officer held the other. Fortunately the body was by now quite stiff and he slid gradually down into our grasp as the ligature was cut at a point between the neck and the branch. He was lowered onto his back, the ligature being cut again at a point well away from the knot; it was important to preserve the knot for examination by the forensic scientists - this would prove whether the victim could have secured it himself. Not satisfied with retaining just the knot, it was also decided that a section of the tree branch should be removed as evidence - if only someone had a saw! The photographer was now allowed to take photographs without revealing our 30 minutes of inactivity when the corpse had been blowing about freely in the breeze!

I felt by now that my knowlege of hangings had been advanced sufficiently for me to return to my own patch and I went to walk away from the scene; but I had only walked a short distance when I heard the immortal words carried on the wind!

"I think it would be very good experience for PC Houlton to deal with this one, sir." One of the kind CID officers was volunteering me for the task and for those unfamiliar with police jargon, I will translate what he really meant - 'I don't see why I should deal with a messy hanging when there is a young constable available to do it instead!' I was to hear this phrase time and time again throughout my service but as I always relished a challenge, I was usually prepared to accept it. I often wondered how many of these so-called 'experienced officers' had ever dealt with similar incidents themselves - it certainly was an excellent way of avoiding work and had the bonus of appearing at the same time to be being generous in helping others to advance their careers!

The doctor duly arrived to pronounce life extinct, whereupon a search commenced of the deceased's pockets. Quite unusually, there was no wallet or other item which would lead us to his identity. The number of officers at the scene gradually dwindled to two, myself and the detective sergeant, who was as bewildered as I was concerning this lack of identification. The labels from his clothing had all been removed and the only item in his trouser pockets was a bunch of door keys. I made out a list of his few personal possessions and placed them into a plastic bag and labeled it; whilst his wedding ring and spectacles presented no problems, his false teeth certainly did. At the best of times someone else's false teeth are bad news - the first time an undertaker calmly removes them from a dead body and hands them to you, it is a little unnerving. Although we did not appreciate it at the time, the spectacles and dentures were the objects which would eventually lead to the identity of our man.

The undertaker manoeuvered the 'shell', a temporary metal box the size of a coffin, into position alongside the body and the three of us lifted the dead man in. The lid was then secured. You may recall that we were standing on a severe slope to the pathway below. Now this 'shell' had many of the characteristics of a sledge and the ground had the firmness of packed snow covered with the lubricant of wet grass and fallen leaves. It was impossible to carry the shell because of the slope, so it was decided to use gravity to our advantage, by holding the side handles and steering it as best we could. The three of us mustered all of our strength, rather like a tug of war team laying on the rope. All was well for a few yards until the undertaker lost his footing and the shell gathered speed with the two of us holding on for dear life until by chance, a small sappling stood in our path and obliged us by bending almost flat as the shell hit it. We slithered on down the slope in this same fashion and I remember wondering what Monsieur Clouseau, alias Peter Sellers, would have made of our efforts? If we were portrayed as the best police force in the world, I thought, God help the rest!

The small section of tree with the rope still attached was placed in the CID van to be taken to my home, which also doubled as a small village police station. I was careful to place it well away from the wood used to light my coal fires! The usual lines of enquiry were set in motion to discover the identity of what was now 'my body'. The local newspapers were asked to publish details of his clothing and the description included his approximate age, height, etc. In most cases this achieves the desired result quickly, with concerned friends or relatives ringing the station within a few hours, but we had no such luck this time. The phones were ominously silent that evening and by the following morning we realised that we would have do some searching ourselves.

One explanation for the lack of response could of course be, we thought, that he lived outside of our area, but the lack of an abandoned vehicle almost ruled this out. The next and more worrying reason might be that he lived alone with no relatives or friends to realise that he was missing. If this was the case, no amount of publicity would enable us to trace him, unless a caring neighbour eventually rang us. The following day I took the spectacles and false teeth to as many opticians and dentists as I could find. A personal visit has certain advantages over a telephone call and within a few hours I struck lucky. The man had been dead for some time before he had been found and together with our further two day delay, by now it was probably closer to three days since he had last been in his home. A dentist checked his records and seemed certain that our corpse was one of his patients. I was amazed that he could match up a set of false teeth so quickly. The address he provided was only two miles from Bath Pool and buoyed with this new confidence, the detective sergeant drove me there immediately. Conclusive proof would be provided if the keys from his pockets fitted the front door of the house!

The property was in the middle of a terrace of pre-war houses with its front door opening directly onto the footpath and the rear door leading to a small yard surrounded by a six foot brick wall. The sergeant took the keys and the first one he tried fitted the front door. The house contained old furniture and smelt very strong and musty. We commenced a search of the ground floor and soon discovered that the owner had clearly loved animals; there were species of birds in cages all around the room; budgerigars of various colours and canaries hopping about excitedly. A cat cowered in one corner clearly bewildered by the presence of strangers and when I opened the back door to get some fresh air, I found further rows of wire cages containing guinea fowl, small ducks and chickens.

The sergeant looked at me and uttered the first words since we had entered the house, "You know all about animals, don't you Constable? Now's your chance to put it into practice. Find the nearest pet shop and get some food for this lot. Goodness knows when they last had a meal - and don't forget to obtain a receipt or you'll never be able to claim it back."

I quickly filled the water containers inside each cage to the obvious delight of the occupants who rushed forward oblivious to my strange presence. The thought suddenly passed through my mind of the suffering they would have endured if our dentist had not led us to the scene.

No note had been left by the deceased, which in modern times makes a coroner reluctant to issue a verdict of suicide in such circumstances; but even then, it makes me wonder how a verdict of misadventure or accidental death can be returned in such cases. How on earth can anyone climb a tree with a dog lead around their neck, tie one end to the branch and then accidentally fall, resulting in them hanging, without forseeing the result? Perhaps there are people who wear wellingtons to climb trees for fun with a dog lead tied around their neck, but I must admit to not seeing many other than those of course who have fallen to their death!

My mission to the pet shop and my return, clutching various brown paper bags of food, went unnoticed by the people in the village. While I was away, the sergeant had busied himself with the task of making a thorough search of the house. Upstairs he had found a collection of antique guns which he thought to be valuable and as such needed to be secured at the police station.

As I concluded my zoo keeping activities, there came a knock on the front door. Word certainly travels fast where bad news is concerned and our visitor turned out to be a man in his sixties announcing that he was a distant relative of the deceased! He was invited inside and in normal circumstances we would have handed the keys to him and given him the responsibility for the safety of the house and its contents; but within a few minutes he was asked to leave - the sergeant was concerned at his interest in the gun collection; he was clearly not interested in anything other than picking over the contents like a vulture. Whilst this behaviour was common, it was usual to wait at least until the police had gone!

The sergeant was concerned that others might also have a claim on the estate and he decided not to hand the keys over to anyone other than our friends from the RSPCA. Eventually the contents were distributed by the solicitors acting for the interested parties and most of the animals were found new homes by the RSPCA. I was pleased because it had concerned me that the animals and birds were not left to the mercy of the caring relatives!

I had learnt a lot from this incident - mostly to avoid taking the advice of those supposedly more experienced at policework than I was!

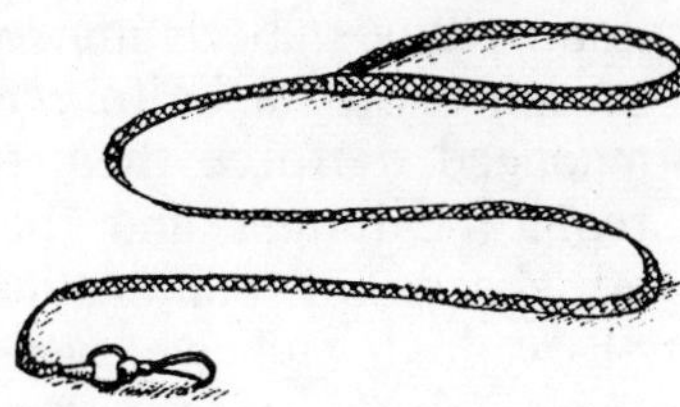

CHRISTMAS AT TALKE PITS

My one man police station at Talke Pits stood in Crown Bank, a road full of exclusive houses, with the station half way down the hill which led to the Main Street. At the back of the house was a large garden which backed onto farmers' fields; on a clear day, you could stand in the garden and see the Welsh mountains.

Three coal fires kept the house aired, which is an accurate description, as not one room became warm in winter. Metal windows ensured that the wind merely slowed down on contact with the house, to become a slight breeze as it passed through the property and out through the windows on the other side. My first mistake was made entirely due to the move taking place in summertime, when glorious sunshine cascaded through the french windows. These were also made of metal and led from the lounge onto a small patio constructed of 3 foot by 2 foot concrete slabs.

It seemed perfectly reasonable on a hot July day to try and open the two doors and allow some fresh air into the room. I was dismayed to find that the previous occupant had foolishly painted all around the doors and frames, both inside and outside, sealing them closed. Much scraping with a knife was needed before with one grand heave, I managed to force them open. Crusts of thick paint fell in lumps from the hinges and the edges of the doors were left with jagged shards of paint sticking out, but I had achieved the result I wanted and we were now able to walk directly from the lounge into the garden. At the end of the day I tidied up the paintwork and made the doors close securely again.

A warm breeze from the Welsh mountains in July is quite different from a February snow storm from the same direction! My family drew my attention to the ice forming on the patio doors and I quickly realised that it was on the inside, not the outside, where it rightfully belonged. Double glazing was in its infancy then but it gave me the idea of placing a large sheet of polythene on the inside, to create a barrier of air between the glass and the occupants of the room. I could feel the wind whistling through the gaps which had previuosly been sealed with layers of paint. Armed with a large sheet of polythene and a roll of sellotape, I decided to put my plan into action. I cut the polythene into three pieces, one to cover the two doors and two smaller pieces to cover the windows to the side of the doors. I placed the first piece against the frame and taped one side in place. I certainly wanted to avoid any wrinkles in the sheet and was careful to keep it taught as the tape was applied. The top and bottom were sealed and the final length of tape was applied to the opposite side.

My fears of having any wrinkles in the finished job were quickly dispelled - as the last inch of tape was fixed to the frame, the whole sheet of polythene tightened up as if it was being blown up like a balloon. Within seconds it had bulged out towards me and appeared at the point of bursting, the wind straining it to its limits. Needless to say, when I tried to fit the larger piece over the doors, no amount of sellotape could hold back the gale which had already travelled so far from Wales to attack my patio doors. All my future decisions in connection with alterations and modifications to the house, would be embarked upon with more care and restraint, I decided!

My colleagues in charge of the other four one-man police stations in the area worked mainly from 9am to 5pm with an occasional late shift on a Friday or Saturday. My enthusiasm, being at its peak, led me to accept working split shifts, unheard of in this modern age of policing, but quite popular in the 1960's. My duty would start at 9am when some of the retired residents of the village could be relied upon to provide useful information over a cup of tea. Then, having worked for the rest of the morning, I would finish duty at lpm. The afternoon would be spent gardening or involved in one of my many little 'sidelines' specifically designed to produce a little extra income. After an evening meal, I returned to duty again at 7pm and continued on patrol until 11pm. This 'split-duty' served to confuse the local villains, who could never be sure that 'the ginger-headed copper' was not just around the next corner.

Christmas day arrived and after the children had opened their presents and breakfast was finished, I decided to visit some of the old people who I knew would be on their own at the festive season. I set off in my uniform to have a 'tipple' with some of these old locals but as I passed the local farmer's home at the bottom of the bank, I made the mistake of agreeing to look at his new colour television, the only one in the area. His idea of a tipple was to pour Bell's whisky into a large tumbler until it reached half an inch from the top - a mouthful of lemonade was added for taste. The whisky went straight to my legs and with a minor headache already coming on, I left the farm and made my way towards the home of a local widow. She added a small sherry to the whisky inside me before I left to walk along the main street in the centre of the village. Even one of the local villains shouted "Merry Christmas" to me as I passed him and the world seemed a very good place.

In the distance, I saw a small group of old ladies standing on the footpath, gazing up at the bedroom window of a terraced house, the front door of which opened directly onto the footpath. As I got nearer, it had not dawned on me that they were going to involve me in their deliberations, but then the nearest one walked slowly towards me.

"I'm sorry to trouble you officer but we are worried about Bill. He lives on his own and we haven't seen him at all this morning." A single bottle of milk stood on the doorstep and the curtains were drawn, preventing any view to the inside of the house.

"Could it just be that he has gone away for Christmas, to stay with friends?" I asked.

"He could have, but we don't think so," came the reply from another elderly lady who had just arrived to swell the growing band outside the house.

Children with new bikes delivered that very morning by Father Christmas, rode back and forward past us, but my thoughts were now on the task in hand. Why on earth had I ventured out on Christmas Day, when I could be sitting warmly with my family?! I must need my head examining; but this was not the time to reflect on such impulsive decisions and in any case, the whisky was now causing little men to bang drums inside my head!

As the moments passed, it became clear that most of the assembled crowd thought that Bill was inside the house and my only course of action would be to break the door down. We have all seen the television programmes where a good kick or a shoulder charge forces a door to open. Well, don't believe all you see! Those doors are made of thin plywood and the locks are designed to fall off at the slightest pressure. The door I faced was made of oak with locks and hinges like those used on church doors in the Middle Ages. My first shoulder charge saw me rebounding off it as though I had run into a brick wall. A succession of similar assaults, during which I used every ounce of my twelve stones on the door, brought a response from one old lady,

"Be careful you don't hurt yourself; those old doors are made to last, not like the modern ones." Humiliation was staring me in the face as I breathlessly replied,

"You are sure he hasn't gone away for Christmas?

The lock eventually gave way and a relieved audience stood back as I entered the house. The kitchen and front room were empty with no sign of Bill. The downstairs rooms were very tidy and the thought that I had damaged the front door of a man on holiday flashed once again through my mind; what on earth would the Inspector make of it all? One of the ladies entered the house and went straight to a small door in the entrance hall.

"I bet he's upstairs," she said, and tried the latch on the door. My heart sank as she announced, "There's a bolt on the other side and it has been fastened. He must be upstairs."

My mind was made up by now that Bill was indeed upstairs. The door must have been bolted from the other side and it began to seem to my mind a classic case of suicide. Christmas is a popular time for this type of incident, when families are together enjoying the festivities and old people get very lonely and depressed. I started to prepare myself for the worst.

My right shoulder was by now too sore to use on this second door and I leaned against the far wall, with my foot near the bottom of the door. The screws holding the bolt gradually eased themselves out of the frame and could be heard falling to the floor on the other side. Not wishing any of the old ladies to see the scene which I now fully expected, I asked them to stay downstairs while I checked the bedrooms.

The staircase was bare wood and the walls were painted in a dark green gloss paint. Ahead, I could see light from the bedroom door which was half open. I entered the room, which was quite warm considering it was wintertime in a type of house not noted for its qualities of insulation. As I reached the entrance to the bedroom, my eyes were drawn to an elecric flex which trailed from the socket right across the room to an electric fire - which was glowing away. The bed appeared to be made up but not slept in and I quickly scanned the room for signs of Bill. My heart sank when I saw his body lying on the floor at the side of the bed, fully clothed, complete with his leather boots and tweed jacket. I could find no sign of pills or vomit, which would be normal in these circumstances. I knelt down beside him to check for a pulse although I was sure in my own mind that there would be none. He was on his side facing me and as I pushed his shoulder back to look at his face, his eyes blinked before opening fully to stare at me. I was slightly shocked but my first aid training took control and I loosened his clothing at the neck and waist. I took his tie off and propped him up against the side of the bed before shouting down to the crowd downstairs and outside, "Get an ambulance, he's alive."

My first aid had never been of text book standard but I could recall the important things - reassure the patient and keep him warm.

"Right Bill, you're OK now, we will have you sorted out in no time."

It sounds a little silly now, but if you had spent many hours lying on the floor then those words would probably be of great comfort to you. For his part, Bill tried to smile to show his appreciation, but it was clear that most of his strength had ebbed away. I gently rubbed his cold hands with mine and covered him with a blanket from the bed. It was still not clear to me what had happened to him and apart from a slight abrasion on his head, I could find no reason for him to be lying on the floor in the first place.

"Any chance you can remember what happened, Bill?" I said, in the hope that he could tell me before the ambulance arrived. He whispered back in short gasps. "Went for a drink yesterday. Came upstairs and fell over that damn wire. Couldn't get up!"

The ambulance arrived and Bill was lifted into one of those strange folding chairs and carried slowly down the stairs into the warmth of the vehicle.

"Lucky you found him," said the ambulance driver. "He couldn't have lasted much longer in this state."

For a moment, I thought to mention the pains that had come in my shoulder, but pride would not let me and anyway I needed to secure Bill's house now and get home to my family. The milk was put into the kitchen, the old ladies were thanked for bringing Bill's plight to my attention and the front door was secured as best as I could in its damaged condition.

As I walked back up the hill to the station, I felt a warm glow inside - despite the fact that the effects of the whisky were wearing off and my headache was coming on worse. Was it coincidence, I wondered, that I had decided to go out on patrol on Christmas Day, when most of the one-man constables would have remained at home with their families? Whatever the explanation, Bill made a full recovery and regularly stopped to have a chat with me from then on. He kept blaming the flex from the fire as the cause of his problems but of course, I had to remark, it was that same fire that had kept him alive for all those hours he had spent lying on the cold floor.

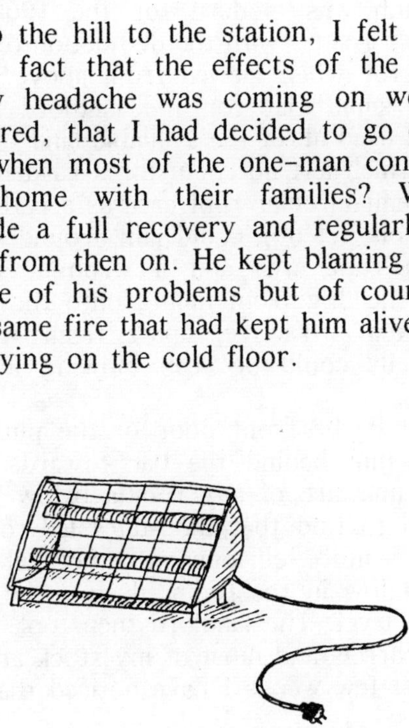

STAKE OUT AT THE PUB

In those days of public houses closing at 10.30pm and constant routine visits after time by the police, it may come as no surprise to learn that I was not welcomed with open arms at such places locally. One sunny summer morning, I was on a leisurely foot patrol around the village when I saw the local licensee brushing out the entrance of his public house.

"Morning," I said, not expecting a great deal of response. To my surprise, he walked across the car park towards me and struck up a conversation.

"I've been hoping to see you for a few days, officer," he started, "I've been having a problem with my stock in the cellar and if you've got time I would like you to see the problem for yourself."

The pub was modern for the 1960s, and sited at the junction of two roads, with the distinction of a round front rather like a protractor when viewed from above. On the second floor there was a small flat for the landlord and his family. The designers had used all of the available land to site the building and its car park which left no room for a garden - the answer was to use the flat semi-circular roof area as a patio where clothes could be dried and his pet dog could run around. A door from the flat led onto the roof area and a wrought iron fence prevented children and the dog from falling onto the car park. The design certainly looked attractive, apart from wash days, when the landlords smalls could be seen blowing in the wind for miles around!

I entered the front door of the pub behind the landlord and followed him behind the bar towards a flight of concrete steps. I was unaware of any rooms below the ground floor and was surprised to find that the stairs led to a store room below the bar. Even more curious was the fact that sunlight shone through a window in the room, despite the fact that it appeared below ground level. The landlord then took up the story.

"The barrels and most of my stock are kept down here but during the last few weeks I have noticed that some small items

have gone missing. I don't think that it's my staff, as it would be easier for them to take from behind the bar. I think someone is using that window over there to take things." I looked through the window which had metal bars set into the brickwork, rather like a prison cell.

"It's the only fault I can find with the pub," said the licensee, "but the room is so small that things must be stacked near to that window, I have no other choice."

I pressed my face up to the bars and saw that the designers had built a narrow pathway behind the store and excavated the the earth to allow natural light into the room. The distance between the bars was only about 2 inches and there was no glass or indeed any window frame. Cigarettes were piled high in packets of 20s, 10s and some 5s - those were indeed the good old days when shopkeepers were prepared to split a packet of five and sell cigarettes in singles - good news for people like me who were trying to give up but saw no harm in buying just one. I could go all day without a cigarette, consoled by the thought that I would reward myself at about 9pm from the corner shop. By buying only one, it prevented me carrying the other four or nine in my pocket, which would be too great a temptation.

It was quite possible for a hand to pass between the bars

of the window and remove a few packets of cigarettes. The thief could walk down the path and then make his escape undetected within a few minutes. In the modern days of crime prevention officers, the landlord would be advised to fit a frame and unbreakable perspex, thus preventing any recurrence, but I was not interested in merely stopping theft; my word no! I wanted to catch them, in the act if possible! Crime statistics were very important to a village constable as a measure of his success. If this crime was reported and then duly solved, it would go down as a 100% detection rate. The licensee was not sure if any cigarettes had in fact vanished through the window - although he was 99% sure of it. To me this was not enough to initiate recording a crime. If however I did catch someone and he admitted taking cigarettes on two other occasions, then together with the time he was caught, I would be able to record three crimes committed and three cleared up! I am sure you get the picture, but for those who are unsure, let us assume that the local Cooperative store was broken into during the same month and stock worth £5,000 stolen.

Although we all know which crime is more serious and therefore most in need of detection, if we assume that no progress is made with the bigger job, those three detected cigarette thefts make a total of four crimes for the village in one month. The fact that three have been cleared up brings my success rate to a highly commendable 75%. I was very aware of these ways to 'fiddle' the figures, but I was generally fortunate in clearing up every crime reported in the village. This may sound smug but it was the result of many hours of boring observations - who else would get up at 4am to watch for someone who stole bottles of milk from a doorstep!

The licensee was pinning his hopes entirely on my shoulders and I was not going to let him down. It would not be for lack of effort if I failed - this was my big chance to get to know him better. A great deal of things are discussed in pubs and even if he only gave me a few pieces of information in the future, the effort would have been worthwhile. Observations would resolve the matter, I felt certain, and within a few days I was sitting in the storeroom complete with my flask and sandwiches.

Some might think observations boring but if you treat it as if you are an angler setting up his tackle then you won't go far wrong. You know that the big fish must be in the lake somewhere just waiting to take the bait, and it is well worth waiting for days or even weeks for that big tug on the line!

My view out of the window was quite good but the pathway remained annoyingly silent for hours on end. The landlord made several visits and offered to bring me a pint of his best beer on a number of occasions - I was not worried about being under the influence if my prey came into the trap - the main reason for my refusal to partake of his hospitality was fear of a visit by my sergeant or worse still, the Inspector. What would they have made of me, sitting in the cellar of a pub drinking a foaming pint of beer? But to be honest, in the 1960s, some senior policemen made a habit of calling in at public houses, mainly by the back door! Looking back, I have no doubt that they would have just stayed with me for a while - at least until the landlord came down to bring them a drink as well. I think I must just have been a little naive at the time!

In order to make the task a little easier for the would-be thief, I placed several packets of 10s of cigarettes on the window ledge within easy reach of the window. My trap was set but the hours and days passed without result and I was beginning to think that the landlord could have been wrong and either no cigarettes had been taken or they had vanished from behind the bar after all. Just as I thought of calling it a day and concluding my observations, I heard the sound of footsteps below the window. I listened intently for a few seconds before a hand appeared through the bars. I remained motionless as it groped along the sill and located a packet of cigarettes only inches from my face. Although I could see the hand, there was no sign of a head or any other part of the body. Indeed the hand seemed at full stretch as its finger tips moved the packet towards the bars.

Despite allowing for almost any eventuality; taking food with me, a torch and handcuffs; I had failed to take account of one serious detail. The time had arrived for me to take positive action and the full realisation of my predicament struck home as I reached forward and grabbed the wrist. The culprit was in my grasp but he, or she, was outside the pub and I was well and truly inside, with metal bars between us! These were pre-radio days which prevented me making an urgent call for assistance. I took a firm hold of the wrist expecting a considerable amount of resistance but it was far less than expected. Although I was by now on my feet with my face as close to the bars as possible, all I could see was the top of a head. I pulled with all of my strength, lifting the culprit level with the window and into my view. He was certainly in a state of shock and he didn't utter a word as our eyes met. He was about 12 years old and not at all what I was expecting. His wrists were too small for handcuffs and even though he was only slightly built there was no way that I could hold him in mid-air for much longer.

In everyone's life there are times when inspiration is needed and my next move must rank in that category. I looked straight at him and said, "I know your dad and he is not going to be very pleased about this, is he? I am going to lower you back to the ground and then I will come round for you. Don't you dare move from that spot."

I ran through the pub leaving a startled group of drinkers looking in disbelief. There was certainly no time for explanations, especially if the young man had decided to take to his heels. All that time spent for nothing, just because I didn't think far enough ahead! By the time I reached the back of the pub, I was breathless but to my amazement the boy was standing there, as good as gold just as I had told him.

It was difficult to feel bad about him in these circumstances - and even more difficult to take him home when I had no idea who he was or where he lived. I overcame this problem, without revealing my secret by saying, "You lead the way; I know the landlord of the pub and perhaps we can come to some arrangement about paying for the cigarettes you have taken in the past." And in this manner, I kept his mind diverted from the fact that I was always a yard behind him as we walked through the housing estate to confront his dad!

I knew that the boy would not be dealt with by the Courts, even if I did hours of paperwork. It certainly did not qualify as the crime of the century, but I knew I had now made a friend for life in the landlord. I could certainly be sure of some information from him in the future and the boy's father was next in line, I thought, to become an extra pair of eyes for me. My approach was simple. I explained the circumstances and then said I would use my influence with the landlord to keep matters quiet, providing the boy paid for the missing stock from his pocket money.

A grateful father thanked me for helping him out of a difficult situation and back I went to the pub to announce the result. A delighted landlord was told to expect payment from the boy's father and I left with a bottle of beer to drink at home - paid for, of course! And I had learnt a valuable lesson for my future observations and would try never again to fall so foul of poor advance planning.

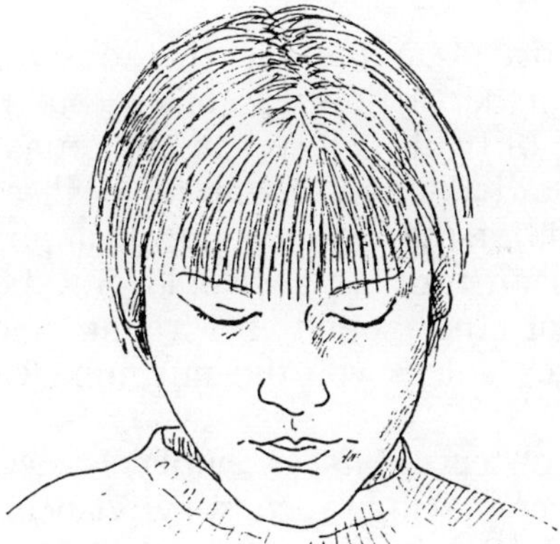

AFTER HOURS DRINKING

Although I had my own police station at Talke Pits, I was often used to supplement the staff at Kidsgrove, particularly if observations were required at night. This allowed the main station to continue operating with a full complement of men and it was thought that the villagers would not notice my absence for a few nights.

A report of alleged late night drinking had been received, no doubt from some disgruntled local who had not been invited to join the all-night fun! Many such letters and anonymous phone calls were received, sometimes even from wives who wished to see more of their husbands, but not all were acted upon. The complaint in question seemed fairly detailed and accurate, giving precise details of times drinking took place and how many people took part.

It was recorded in the file that observations were to be kept before any further action was taken, but the public house in question would be difficult to keep an eye on as it stood on a long winding lane miles from any form of civilisation. High hedges enclosed either side of the lane, making it impossible to hide from passing cars when on foot; there would only be a few seconds to dive for cover at the sound of a car and then only into impenetrable hedges unless you did not mind getting your clothes ripped to pieces.

Normally, observations on public houses would start with a uniformed officer having a cursory glance as he passed the premises on patrol. But it was clear to me that any sighting of a uniformed officer in that lane would immediately reach the ears of the landlord - the lane led from Bath Pool to Green's slaughterhouse about a mile past the pub and there would be no reason for a foot patrol to be wandering about in the lane after dark.

"It is entirely up to you how you go about it, Houlton," the sergeant said, handing me the letter. "Just come back in a few days with basic information; you know - are the lights on after midnight? Are people entering and leaving after closing time? Can you hear the sound of the till being used? Are glasses clinking in the early hours?"

Observations are often boring and this job seemed no different from the rest; cold nights and inactivity for hours with the thought all the time that you could be at home tucked up in bed, warm and comfortable. I had cause to drive past the pub to Green's slaughterhouse to sign their movement of animals book and this gave me the chance to have a closer look at the lay-out of the pub in daylight; to see where the doors were located, etc. Although you think that you can remember what a place looks like, it often bears little resemblance when you try to draw it accurately on paper. My past experience of drawing sketch plans of scenes of accidents in the police station and then returning to take accurate measurements, told me that, more often than not, the sketch bore no resemblance to the actual road lay-out. You can drive past a road junction every day but when asked to draw the position of the road signs or central line markings, if any, then you start guessing.

I drove slowly past the public house, in order to collect as much information as possible, knowing that what I missed on the run out to Green's could be resolved on the way back along the lane. It was just what I needed; it showed me that the front entrance was by way of a small brick porch in the centre of the building with the main door opening onto the lane. The toilets were outside, to the right hand side of the main building, forcing those with weak bladders to regularly leave the pub by the main front door and walk some 20 yards. To the left of the main building was what appeared to be a detached brick garage, no doubt for the landlord's private use.

Across the lane from the public house was a gap in the hedge allowing access, by way of two large wooden farm gates, into two fields separated by a further hedge. The fields were grassed and the ground level rose up for a distance of about half a mile. It was perfect for making observations. What I did not notice was a shallow ditch which separated the two fields and ran alongside the dividing hedge - the ditch carried water, but not the crystal clear spring type stuff written of in poems. No babbling over shiny stones glinting in the early morning sun for this stream! No, this was more your slurry stream from the third world, consisting of thick black mud, forming stagnant pools with a topping of green algae. It was the type of stream which was best avoided even by gnats and flies!

I returned home to Talke Pits to make more detailed plans, including the layout drawing and dates when I would be able to devote all of my time to the project; to include, for instance:

Time of arrival - not later than 11pm.
Time of departure - not before 2am (unless things go quiet)
Method of entry - by way of front door
Cover exits - to be checked

Should the information turn out to be malicious then the licensee would remain unaware of our activities and the letter could be filed safely with those labelled mischief makers, revenge or grudge complaints!

My location for the observations was to be the rising ground in the field opposite the public house, where no one could see me apart from the odd wandering cow. My uniform was discarded to be replaced with a pair of old jeans, a warm jumper and a thick overcoat. My approach to the field would be by the lane after being dropped off by the police car about half a mile away by the entrance to Bath Pool. I would walk up the lane and trust that any passing traffic would regard me as just another drinker making his way to the public house.

You may well wonder why I did not just go into the pub as a customer and wait to see if they allowed me to stay on after time. This is a perfectly reasonable question with a very easy answer. The Beatles were then at their most popular complete with long sideburns and great mops of hair. Everyone of my age copied this modern look except young police officers who had almost shaven heads! Even when out of uniform, it stood out like a sore thumb and you could only be a policeman or a member of the armed forces on leave!

The night chosen for my first visit happened to be one of those cloudless moonlit nights when your vision becomes good after only a few minutes away from artificial lighting. I alighted from the police car and started walking uphill along the lane, trying to look as natural as possible. Only one vehicle went past me and as he was heading back towards the town, I knew that it was unlikely that he would notice anything out of the ordinary. The driver had slowed down to pass me and as his headlights held me in full view, I raised an arm to acknowledge his thoughtfulness. As I neared the public house, I could hear the sound of voices being carried on the night air. The front door then closed and I could just hear the muffled sound of many voices inside. Drink does make people talk in loud voices and there seemed to be many such inside.

Seven or eight cars were parked on the car park and as it was now almost 11pm, they should all have been moving off during the next ten minutes. Licensing hours finished officially at 10.30pm and most pubs had emptied completely by 11pm. I looked towards the the gates which led to the fields and within seconds I had climbed over the left hand one and was making my way up the field, a few yards away from the boundary hedge. The grass was a little damp but I decided to sit down and rest my legs some 30 yards into the field; it could be a long night in view of the obvious activity inside the public house and bearing in mind the good visibility provided by the moon, it was only sensible to keep as much of my frame out of sight as possible.

I had a good view of the front door where a porch light illuminated all those who came or left. All of the windows had thick curtains drawn across them but they could not prevent glimmers of light showing through all the ground floor ones. It was silent except for brief muffled voices each time someone opened the front door to visit the lavatory. I could just make out the noise of flushing each time they returned to the warmth of the pub.

A glance at my watch in the moonlight told me that I had been there for about an hour, and not one customer had left to go home. It certainly seemed that my time was not being wasted and that our informant had briefed us well. The only justifiable reason for the landlord keeping such hours would be that he was holding a private party for invited guests, with the premises closed to the public and no payment made for drinks. This excuse was often put forward in Court and usually the publican was given the benefit of the doubt. My job was to prove that 'private parties' happened most nights and that the licensee took after the Queen in having more than one birthday each year!

I made some notes in my pocket book and then looked up towards the public house, just in time to see the silhouette of a woman in a headscarf standing by the gate at the entrance to the field. She bent down but I was unable to see what she was doing until she stood up again. Who on earth would bring two labrador dogs and release then into a field at midnight? She was doing exactly that, which filled me with horror. I decided to sit tight in the hope that the dogs would remain near to the gate, have a quick sniff, cock a leg and return to their owner. My hopes were dashed as they both wandered closer and closer to me. How on earth could I hide from two dogs whose very nature is to seek out recently shot birds in open country? Instinct told me that I must move slowly towards the cover of the hedge where the land dipped towards the brook. I was soon crawling, legs first into the evil liquid which I had not noted in my planning and this only served to attract the attention of the nearest dog, who raised his head and looked straight at me. For several seconds he stayed in that position, totally motionless and then his head moved from side to side as if trying to identify what I was. His owner was by now calling him, "Buster; Jessie." If only he would do as he was told and go home like a good boy, but Buster was having none of it. Without moving any closer to me he suddenly started to bark, loud enough to wake the dead. The dog was not going to stop until I took some kind of action and so I climbed up out of the ditch, covered in mud.

I strode towards the lady with the dog still barking continuously behind me. When I reached a position some ten yards from the owner, I said in a firm voice, "I am sorry if I have startled you, but I am a police officer. You must not say anything about what you have seen tonight. Your cooperation will be much appreciated. Please take your dogs home."

She called both dogs to her side and fastened them on leads before walking off down the lane. She did not say a word to me and as far as I am aware, she did not contact the police station to check that I was genuine. By sheer luck not one person emerged from the public house while all of this took place and I quickly returned to my vantage point in the field where I remained until about 3am. Only a few customers left during this period and I estimated that there were at least ten die-hards left inside even then.

I returned to Kidsgrove Police Station and completed a short report outlining what had taken place, feeling sure that when the night Sergeant read it he would authorise a raid within days. To my dismay, he concluded that it could have been just a 'one-off' incident and no raid could even be contemplated until a pattern of late night drinking had been established!

My counterpart at Talke Police Station, some mile and a half from my own Station, was entrusted with the following nights' observations and as I was keen to ensure that he did not fall victim to dog bites, I went to see him the next afternoon and discussed my encounter with the dogs. I am sure that he will not mind me mentioning his name because I always thought of PC Graham Fletcher as a shining example to all young officers of the day. He was always undeniably calm and collected, dealing with every one equally and fairly. He had a passion for playing musical instruments and he would hum tunes as he worked. He always seemed very content and happy with his lot!

He listened to my tale of woe over a cup of tea and when I eventually left him, I felt sure that he was prepared for anything, although not thrilled at the prospect of spending five hours in open countyside. But there was nothing more I could do and as it was my rest day - and badly needed at that, I left it with him. When I returned to duty and telephoned Kidsgrove two days later, I was more than slightly shocked to hear that poor old Graham was recuperating at home, having injured his legs whilst on the observations. I went straight round to his home where I was greeted by his wife.

"Come in Trevor," she said, leading me to the front room where Graham was sitting in an armchair with his legs raised on a stool. Both were heavily bandaged and clearly causing him considerable pain. I wanted to blurt out something like, "I told you about those dogs, why didn't you listen to me?" but I kept my composure and asked him what had happened. With hindsight, I am glad that I had waited - no one could have predicted what he then said.

"It all happened so quickly, Trevor. My shins are really sore," he went on. "I've got to keep my legs elevated for a few days; I'm not even allowed to get up and make a drink." I interrupted him, unable to contain my curiosity any longer.

"Was it both of the dogs?" I questioned.

"It wasn't the dogs. I am not that stupid. I kept clear of the fields and stood in the entrance of the garage in the car park."

"Well how did it happen," I interrupted him impatiently again.

"The doors were open to the garage, so I stood near to the entrance making sure that no one could see me. A car came down the lane and I stepped back into the garage to avoid being seen in the headlights. I couldn't see inside, and suddenly I fell into this concrete pit. As I fell the front edge took the skin right off my shins - and its bloody painful!" he moaned.

I was tempted to burst out laughing but one glance at the worried look on his wife's face told me that now was not the time or place to see the funny side of things. I wished him a speedy recovery and left, realising that all future observations were now down to me.

After a further week of watching, it was clear that any planned raid would have to take place on a Friday or Saturday in order to catch the maximum number of miscreants. As I fed my briefings back to the sergeants at Kidsgrove, it also became clear that each one was reluctant to have the raid take place during his period on duty. This was quite understandable as public house raids were not an everyday exercise at small stations and as a result, things could easily go terribly wrong, leaving everyone with egg on their faces!

The next Friday, I took up my position in the field again and using my new issue radio, I sent a message back to the sergeant that around thirty people were still inside the pub drinking at midnight. I expected him to round up all the available officers on duty and hit the place there and then, but it was not to be; the questions flowed from my radio..... "Is the main door open for us to get inside?" "Can you confirm that money is changing hands?" "Are people actually drnking?" Despite confirming all the points put to me, it became obvious to me that the sergeant was not going to 'jack-up' a raid.

"I have just checked the strength on duty and we haven't got the men to cover a job like this and still answer routine calls. It can't go ahead tonight."

Why he had not checked before I went out two hours earlier is a mystery, but I was not in a position to argue. He was in charge and his decision was final!

The following morning I decided to put some pressure on the night sergeant to take positive action and I knew it had to come from above. I typed out a report outlining all of the time that had been expended on the observations to date and recommending urgent action in order to bring the operation to a satisfactory conclusion. The Inspector ensured that men from Newcastle were available to take over the routine patrol, and the sergeant was instructed to supervise the raid which was to take place on the Saturday night. Plans were drawn up for special constables to be on duty from 10pm, to take part in a 'special operation'. Apart from a few people directly involved, it is usually unwise to tell anyone the exact nature of such a job because of the 'jungle telegraph' which might easily reach the ears of the landlord. In this case, the members of the CID were also kept in the dark about the operation, although I had some misgivings about this in view of their nocturnal drinking habits!

I made my way along the lane once more, this time with the smug feeling that at last we were going to show our teeth and bring the matter to a conclusion. Before leaving we had all seen an internal plan of the public house which had been divided into sectors. The bar had three sides allowing drinks to be served to customers in all areas and although the lay-out could be described as open plan, there were secluded corners where drinkers could be missed. Each officer was allocated a small area where he would identify those drinking and obtain a sample of the liquid being consumed. The sergeant would find the landlord and take him to the living quarters where he would be cautioned for any offences disclosed.

My instructions were to establish that there were people inside drinking; that money was changing hands and more important still, that the front door was not locked. As I neared the public house, I was aware that a lot depended on me and that both glory or ridicule were possible outcomes. A small gap in the curtains allowed me to glimpse inside, establishing the fact that the premises were more popular than some public houses during legal opening hours! My hands were slightly clammy as I approached the main door and clasped the door knob. This is it I thought as I made my way back down the lane to join the assembled group of officers at the entrance to Bath Pool.

"It's on, Sarge; the front door is not locked and the place is full to bursting!" I said.

Within seconds we were all strung out in single file walking briskly towards the public house, with me at the head and the sergeant bringing up the rear. What a sight we must have looked - straight out of a 'Carry On' movie!

I was apprehensive as I turned the door knob for the second time that night and the adrenalin flowed as the door swung open and I had my first glimpse into the smoke filled room. I was in my jeans and jumper so my entry into the room did not arouse too much interest and I turned to the right to take up my position at the far end of the room. Within seconds the string of dark blue uniforms was funnelling its way inside and the mood of the drinkers changed from one of noisy joviality to one of stunned silence.

By now I was nearing my designated area at the end of the room near to the open coal fire. There were four tables near the roaring fire, all occupied by customers. It was a dark corner of the pub but the fire lit it sufficiently to recognise faces. Although taken by surprise and with their reactions dulled by alcohol, the drinkers soon started to sober up and appreciate the consequences of what was taking place. The place was a hub of activity with uniformed officers everywhere. Glasses full of frothy beer were quickly declared as 'dead' by people sitting right behind them. I was quickly realising that convicting people of drinking alcohol after closing time was not as easy as it seems -think of the last time you entered a public house and had a quick look around; how many people had a glass of beer actually in their hand? In reality most people are sitting around chatting and smoking with their beer on the table. Although you know in your own mind that a few moments ago they had the glass to their lips, it is not good enough evidence. The drinkers were wise to this move and they pushed the glasses as far away from them as possible. Although there was literally gallons of half drunken beer and spirits on tables and in alcoves, there was no one who would own up to being the drinker of any of it!

"That one was left by a bloke who went at about a quarter past ten officer," came the cocky reply. At the end of the raid it was only possible to take one person to Court for drinking after time!

To my dismay, even worse was about to happen as I scanned the faces of those sitting near to the fire. I recognised a female customer as a special constable and as I tried to establish what she was drinking, a tirade of abuse flowed from her mouth. When I turned towards her, she stood up with her glass held high in front of her.

"There's your bloody evidence," she shouted, and she threw the contents right into the fire. I expected a loud hissing sound as the liquid landed on the flames but quite the opposite happened. Her drink was a double measure of spirit and it had the same result as throwing petrol onto the fire. It reminded me of a fire-eaters act, illuminating the whole room for a few seconds with an intense yellow flame. The woman placed her empty glass on the table and sat down to compose herself again.

"You can collect your uniform whenever you like and you can tell the inspector to shove his whistle up his a....," she ranted. I think I had grasped the crux of this one-sided conversation - she no longer wished to serve in the special constabulary! Not wishing to rub salt into the wound, I marked her down as having an empty glass!

Names were taken and samples of drink poured into containers and labelled and then customers were allowed to leave until only the police officers remained. The Sergeant appeared with a worried looking landlord who was told, "The facts will be reported."

With only one conviction for drinking after hours, it might seem that the whole episode was a waste of time and effort. Far from it! Word spread like wildfire that the Kidsgrove Police were cracking down on licensing offences. Landlords were shocked that such a raid had been conducted on their doorstep - they could quite easily be the next, and routine visits to public houses became for a long time, pleasant affairs with rarely any breaches of the rules.

But from my point of view, the wise old sergeants had been quite right in not wishing to become involved in such an 'enterprise'. Pitfalls lay around every corner just waiting for the unwary to fall into them. It was a number of years before I was involved in another such raid on a public house and you can be sure that the plans for that one were impeccable. The saying that you learn by your mistakes is very true in the police force!

PROWLERS

There were two important books in every police station at this time and these were always the first to be examined during any inspection. The first was the 'Void House' file and the second, the 'Complaint' file. Both were looseleaf. The first was supposed to contain full details of all houses reported as being unoccupied and the second, a list of current complaints by members of the public. If you went on holiday, you would visit your local police station and fill in the top section of a form, containing your address, the dates it would be unoccupied and where you could be contacted in an emergency. The lower part of the form made provision for visiting officers to enter the time and dates when they checked that all was well. When the relevant dates had elapsed, the form was withdrawn from the file. It was one of those caring touches which made the public regard us as the 'best police force in the world'. The file was taken down on night duty and when things fell quiet at around 3am, the officer would drive or walk to all of the addresses listed and mark them off as secure. During the summer months, it helped the time go quickly, and gave a focus to a night shift.

There were country houses on the list which to a humble policeman seemed straight out of Country Life magazine. Grand outdoor pools, tennis courts and glimpses of antique furniture. I recall one officer who was particularly fond of horticulture, returning to the station wide-eyed at finding some rare plant growing in abundance in the grounds of a 'void house'. Discussion with the sergeant ended up in a decision to get the police car out the following night and armed with a trowel and two largish flower pots, they set out to plunder some of the rare plant. Their consciences were pacified by the thought that no one would miss two small pieces of root from such a large specimen.

I watched them leave the station at just after 4am when only milkmen and thieves were about and a couple of hours later I heard the full story of their exploits with much amusement. On their arrival at the isolated house, they drove down the long tarmac drive to a position near to the garage and then to make doubly sure that the owners had not returned, they walked around the house and gardens checking windows and doors. The upstairs curtains were not drawn which was a sure sign that the place was empty. They removed the plant pots from the boot and armed with their trowel, they went towards the plant. Some soil was dug up from around the base to cover the bottom of the plant pots, then one officer held a pot while the other dug a small piece of root from the base of the specimen. The pot was filled with more soil and then the process was repeated with the second pot.

All seemed to be going according to plan when lights suddenly shone from the road illuminating the guilty pair. The plant pot was dropped in the confusion and the soil was scattered on the drive. How were they to have known that the owners were caravan fanatics who after a wet week's holiday had decided to miss the daytime traffic and drive home through the night!

The owners seemed quite surprised to find that the local constabulary were so concerned about their property that they not only sent an officer to check it but also a sergeant as a back-up! I don't know if the owners realised what had been taking place; the culprits were keen to suggest to me that while the owner parked his car they had managed to drop the pots back into the boot unseen and kick the pile of soil under the bushes. I have my doubts about the owner being quite so gullible!

The complaints file was similar to the void house list in that there was a section for the complainant's name and address, then a space to record visits and finally a section to be completed to finalise the form. A member of the public would complain about a problem such as lads playing football in the street and this usually resulted in an initial visit. If it seemed to the constable that other visits would be required to solve the matter, then the form was commenced. As well as ensuring that the problem was not forgotten by other members of the station, it was a record confirming visits at specified times, together with the officer's name. On occasions the form would be littered with visits but on close inspection, the times of the visits seemed suspiciously designed to ensure that all would be quiet - PC Smith was surely unlikely to find boys playing football in the street at 7am!

Although Talke Pits was a 'one-man' station, I was still required to complete these various forms and ensure that visits were made to the various areas of difficulty but I found it easy to remember each complaint and if a visit was made, I would often knock on the door of the complainant to show him something was being done. I recall visiting one such house in Queen Street where the houses were one long terrace. I knocked on the door and was greeted by a small boy about 6 years of age.

"Is your mummy or daddy in please?" I asked, fully expecting him to close the door and go and fetch one of them. Nothing of the sort; he no doubt had had the usual school visit from a policeman keen to show children that the police were his friend - the 1960s were a time of transition from being afraid to even speak to an officer of the law, to actually stopping and asking him questions. The boy was a confident young man who, on seeing my uniform and coming from a good home, was keen to assist me. He opened the door and said "Come in, my mum is here."

Without thinking much about it, I followed him in. The front door led straight to the staircase and on the left was the door into the main room. I followed him into this room to find the usual carpet square in the middle of the floor, some basic furniture and the obligatory large mirror hanging over the fireplace. The fireplace held a roaring coal fire and his mother, who had not yet noticed me, faced the mirror brushing her hair. But I had certainly noticed her! With only hot water available from a kettle in those days, most people in such streets washed in the kitchen sink and this night was no exception. She had stripped down as far as her waist and was now brushing her wet hair in front of the fire. For a few seconds, which did not last nearly long enough as far as I was concerned, I had a perfect view through the mirror of what I judged to be very firm size 36C things! I stood slightly transfixed until to my dismay the boy walked over to his mother and tugged her skirt.

"Mummy; there's a policeman to see you." She turned around to face me, which made it very difficult to maintain eye contact with her! Then she reacted in the same way that some women do when they find a spider walking towards them; she screamed at the top of her voice and blurted, "Get out! Get out!" several times.

The reality of my situation dawned upon me and despite the fact that I had been invited in, I thought now was not the time to discuss the matter further. I left very quickly, thinking what on earth the small boy would make of things - I hope he did not think that grown-ups never allowed policemen into their homes at all!

Prowlers were a comman complaint reported in the complaints book, although many were imagined or linked to a perfectly legitimate explanation. One such complaint of prowlers, from a lady in the village, caused me to complete a form, because it had happened on a regular basis and late at night. I made several visits but never got to the bottom of it. She said that there were noises in her backyard, at 2am and 3am in the night and that, in the morning, she found things disturbed in the garden shed, although nothing was stolen.

It was of some concern to me that despite my best efforts, the file was still open, leading me in the end to discuss the problem with some of her neighbours They knew nothing of the problem, or even that she had complained to the police, but one evening my ears pricked up when during a casual conversation, a man I trusted said,"Have you been watching the yard where Mrs .... lives?"

"Yes, why do you ask?" I answered.

"You are wasting your time if you ask me. She has got a boyfriend you know. Sometimes she wants him and other times she doesn't," came his reply.

This snippet of information made me feel rather foolish. Fancy me being duped by some woman who is using me, a police officer, to sort out her courting problems. It was more than I could stand; I returned to the station and collected the complaint form. Reading the number of fruitless visits made my blood start to boil. How dare anyone deliberately waste my time like this! I strode to the front door of her house with a purpose and banged the knocker loudly. The door opened and I was face to face with the lady.

"You have complained numerous times about prowlers in your yard late at night." She held the front door half open and replied,

"Yes, that's right."

I went straight for the 'jugular', "Don't let us play about. We both know who it is in your yard; it's your boyfriend. If you fancy him one night, you let him in and all is rosy but if you don't fancy him the next, you throw him out. I assume that if he has had too much to drink, he isn't much use to you and out he goes! He hangs about and sleeps in the shed and, to make sure he doesn't bother you, you report a prowler to me. Well, I have better things to do with my time than deal with your courting problems. I am marking this form off accordingly and I will not respond in future."

I waited a second for a reaction but she just stood there dumbfounded. Suddenly to my great surprise the door was pulled open to its full extent. It was a man in his early 30s who in an instant started shouting, "I heard all of that; you have no right to say that, I am going to complain to your sergeant."

Quite clearly he was the boyfriend and in a funny sort of way I was glad it was his day for some hanky-panky or he would only have heard my explanation secondhand. As it was, he had heard the truth from my lips and I felt happy that justice had been done. It was about 10.30pm and time, I thought, that I made my way back to the station.

As far as I was concerned the matter had been concluded in a fair and reasonable manner, but he was having none of it. As I walked away towards the station, I had only gone some 50 yards when I was aware that he was right behind me, having stopped just to put on a coat. He continued our conversation.

"I am going to complain about you. You can't just say things like that and get away with it. I am going to make a complaint to the sergeant in charge."

His words made me feel a little smug inside - if he thought that by following me to Talke Pits police station he would be able to meet a sergeant he was in for a shock.

"I am the one in charge of the station; there is no sergeant, so it is pointless you following me there because there will be no-one there but me. If you don't like hearing the truth, you shouldn't listen behind doors!" I told him firmly and confidently. Despite this, he still followed me right to the door of the station. and as I put the key into the lock, I said, "You might as well go home - I am going to bed." Even this did not deflect him and he followed me into the main office. Clearly, to pacify him I needed to let him speak to the sergeant on the telephone, if he could be located. Luckily when I rang Kidsgrove, he was in the office and I related the story to him with the boyfriend listening to the conversation.

"He says he wants to complain about me, Sarge. I have wasted a lot of time on his girlfriend's prowler and now I want to go to bed. He is standing next to me in the office and says that he won't go until he has spoken to you." The sergeant told me to hand the phone to the boyfriend at that stage. The boyfriend did not say many words and when he put the phone down I asked, "What does he suggest?" "He says that I have to go to Kidsgrove to complain in person, and that is exactly what I am going to do!"

At least this would get rid of him, I thought, and allow me to go to bed, but as he walked out of the station I was suddenly beginning to feel a little uneasy because the sergeant would no doubt bring matters to the attention of the Inspector who might frown upon the blunt way I had handled matters. Kidsgrove was about five miles away and the journey both ways on foot would take him about two and a half hours. This could affect him in one of two ways; he would either calm down, or it would make him even more determined to press his case. I drifted off to sleep and woke at around 8am, finding myself anxious to know what had happened. A phone call to Kidsgrove drew a blank from the station constable.

"No, I can't find anything in the book about it, Trevor, and the sergeant finished duty at 6am. You will have to wait until he comes back on duty and speak to him."

Being kept in suspense for a whole day was not my idea of fun and despite a busy schedule my mind kept returning to the complaint form. At the stroke of 10pm, I was back on the phone to Kidsgrove.

"Can I speak to the sergeant about last night?" I said. After a couple of minutes, the friendly voice of the sergeant came on the line.

"Not another problem, I hope Trevor?"

"No Sarge, I just wondered what happened last night to that chap who wanted to make a complaint about me?" I said, trying not to sound too concerned.

"Oh him. Yes he walked it down here at about 12.45am. You didn't mention that his breath smelled of drink. He came shouting his mouth off disturbing us all," the sergeant went on.

"Did you make out a formal report of his complaint?" I asked.

"No need for that Trevor; I told you he smelled of drink. As soon as he started to moan and groan and tell me what had happened, I said you had done the right thing in telling his girlfriend what you thought about her behaviour. He carried on complaining and I told him if he continued, I would throw him out of the station. He carried on and so I did just that. He went down the steps faster than he came up and we didn't hear from him again!"

In my wildest dreams, I would never have thought that the sergeant would throw a complainant out of the station. I dread to think how many discipline forms would be needed today, just to record such an incident. I would guess that at least 200 man hours would be spent taking statements and serving forms! My lady complainant never caused any problems from that day onwards; nor was anymore heard from the boyfriend. For all I know they lived happily ever after!

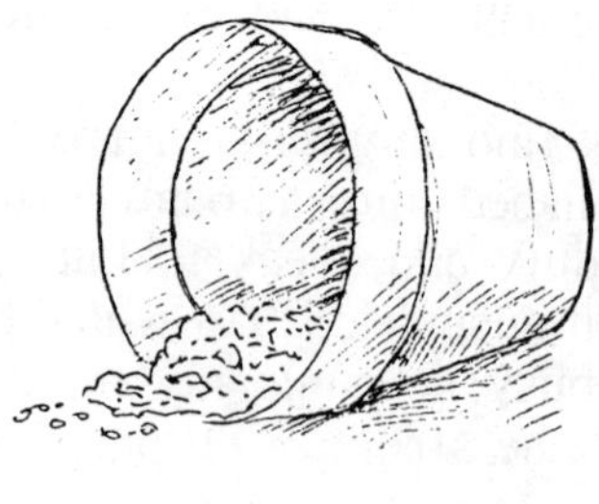

A QUIET SUNDAY

Not everyone working at Kidsgrove shared my enthusiasm for getting out and finding wrong-doers. Some preferred to see things drift along in a well ordered fashion without the stresses and strains of actually looking for trouble. No doubt after 20 years, I would mellow and seek to perform an office job, away from the confrontation involved in patrol work, but this was not even mildly evident to me yet!

The Inspector took charge of all prosecutions at Court and young policemen were required to give evidence, even in cases where the accused pleaded guilty. This gave us confidence in the witness box and more importantly, we were seen and heard by the magistrates every week. It would be fair to say that in the present times, there are young officers with 2 years service who have never given evidence in Court at all. Guilty pleas do not require any evidence to be given but in the 1960s, I was in and out of the witness box like a jack-in-the-box, which not only ironed out the problem of being nervous but had the bonus of showing the magistrates that my words could be relied upon. If ten defendants plead guilty and agree with the evidence I have given, in full view of the magistrates, what chance has defendant number eleven who says I am a liar? On this basis, probationary constables developed a certain relationship with the Court and 'Not Guilty' verdicts were few and far between.

Being keen to bring people before the Court did not always endear me to those senior officers who had to present the evidence. It was not popular to have the Court operating after lunch time on a Friday, the day chosen for Kidsgrove cases. I recall standing in the line of officers about to give evidence one day, when the Inspector made his usual check to see that everyone was fully prepared and smartly turned out. He would check that any exhibits were ready to hand and that our pocket books had been written up with all of the necessary evidence. Constable John Warrilow was of a similar nature to myself and equally as keen to see justice done. He was young and like me he relied on instinct to find the bad guys of Kidsgrove.

We stood side by side with a couple of older constables, waiting for the Court inspection. Inspector Frank Allison took one look at the line up and said, "You two are not here again, are you? What problems have you got for me today? Don't you two ever miss a Court?"

Although we were a constant thorn in his side, I think he had a soft spot for both of us, confident that whatever we did in the town, we were only trying to enhance the reputation of his station. I recall being admonished by the Inspector for some indiscretion and accepting the instruction, "Don't let it happen again", before leaving his second floor office. I went into the yard in a bit of a sulk to return to my station at Talke Pits. One of the old timers who had overheard the one way conversation in the Inspector's office called through the window to me from his cosy desk.

"Got a bollocking again, have we?" I was not too downhearted and I gave as good back as I got, "If I never did any work, then I would be like some of you and never get a bollocking, wouldn't I?"

He was silenced by this cutting response and I never thought about the matter for a couple of weeks, until the Inspector's secretary, Rona spoke to me. She was always very helpful and keen to communicate what the Inspector really thought about his young officers.

"I was with the Inspector after he saw you last week," she started. At this stage my heart fell as I realised that even the station cat knew about my telling off! "The windows were all open, you know, and he heard PC Bracking's remarks. When you had both gone the Inspector told me that your reply was perfectly true and he wished he had got more officers willing to take chances in the way you and PC Warrilow do."

This inside information was most welcome despite the fact that the Inspector was not prepared to tell me himself. This stern style of rule was endemic in the Force and is best illustrated by the story of a parade of the 2pm to 10pm shift one Friday. The Inspector had spent many years gaining experience in all aspects of police duties and was NEVER wrong. Even if he was proved to be wrong beyond any shadow of a doubt, it would never be mentioned. On this particular day, we all knew something was not quite right when he ventured from his office before the 2pm parade. The parade was normally supervised by the sergeant who read out all matters of interest, from stolen car numbers, to who would perform crossing duty when the children came out of school. We all remained silent while this took place, writing down the relevant details in our pocket books.

But today there was no sign of the sergeant - we later learned that he had gone off duty sick. The Inspector was thus about to take the parade himself for the first time since his promotion. We all made sure that our uniforms and boots were up to scratch and that our torches worked. At the call 'parade' we stood to attention with our appointments (handcuffs and truncheons) presented at arms length. On the command 'return', these items were stowed away in our pouches and pockets. The various proceedures went smoothly until we were each given our O.P.sheets (Observation Points). As we had no radios in those days, the only means of contacting individual officers was to ring us at public telephone boxes or physically to walk or drive to us. Therefore, in order to know where we would be at a set time, usually on the hour or half hour, each officer was given a sheet with the times and places he must be at set points. He would make the point at the appointed time and remain there for at least ten minutes, after which he could resume his patrol. The points were all near to telephone boxes and the O.P. sheet showed them only as numbers, from 1 to 20, corresponding to a list of points memorised by all officers. If the sheet was lost and fell into the hands of thieves, they would have no idea where the officer was meant to be!

My sheet had been completed by the Inspector who had obviously forseen the advent of the National Lottery, some thirty years prior to its inception! Being unfamiliar with the up to date position of each point, he had listed my numbers using a crystal ball. The first one related to a position at the top of Kidsgrove Bank on our border with Tunstall. It was some four miles away and with the time now 2.20pm I would have great difficulty arriving by 3pm! I felt a little uneasy about breaking into a canter in full uniform but did not want to make a fuss, resigning myself to the fact that I would be late for the first point. It was as I was about to go through the front door that I noticed that the second O.P. was near to a large electrical factory on the Cheshire border, a distance of some nine miles from the first point! A glance at the other locations confirmed my suspicion that the Inspector had no idea where he was sending me. Even if I was on horse back I would never be able to cover the distances involved, let alone deal with the public's problems en route!

I went to the Inspector and said, " Sir, there must be a mistake on my O.P. sheet because the first is near Tunstall and the next one is about nine miles away on the border with Cheshire."

He took the sheet out of my hand and looked at it. After a few seconds silence he looked at me, gave me the sheet back and said, "You use your initiative, PC Houlton."

His words had no meaning to me and I was still trying to work out exactly what he meant when he continued.

"There's big red things called buses out there; you get on one of them."

Could it be true that he wanted me to spend my patrol standing at bus stops in order to travel around Kidsgrove until 10pm? This is exactly what he meant! and instead of altering the numbers to enable me to walk between the points he said, "Go on then. Out on patrol!"

What a day I spent, riding shotgun on the front step of countless buses going from one end of our area and back again. Luckily in those days policemen were welcome to travel free in their uniform, giving good value to the bus company by way of free protection from drunks and the like.

With this attitude of senior officers towards the lowly constable, it will not surprise you to hear of my next little encounter. It was a sunny Sunday morning with only the sergeant and two constables on duty at Kidsgrove. We had a cup of tea just before 6am and as I was to be the one foot patrol, entrusted with the care and protection of the whole town and surrounding countryside, I gathered my belongings and sat waiting for the sergeant to give me my observation point ticket. As he wrote it out, he gave me certain instructions which he made clear were to be adhered to at all cost! He was not interested in me seeking out wrong-doers on this beautiful morning. No, he warned me about the consequences of bringing him in any kind of police work this morning which might possibly interfere with the cooked breakfast prepared for him at home by his wife at 9am. He further stated that this was the one day of the week when he expected peace and quiet in order for him to start a new week fully refreshed.

My reputation for causing work in the station was not in any doubt and to prevent me coming into contact with too many members of the public, my observation points had been arranged accordingly. The first, at 7am, was heading out into the countryside, followed by an 8am point still further miles from civilisation!

I set off with his words ringing in my ears and I was soon walking through fields and woods with only the birds for company. Never mind; I was being paid for being in the fresh air and there would be no writing to do. It was a very enjoyable way to pass the morning and I was contemplating how I would spend the afternoon when out of the silence I heard a loud bang. How often have witnesses related a bang to a car backfiring, only to find that it was a gunshot and they had heard a murder committed? To my mind the bang was indeed associated with a car backfiring some distance away but as I looked up at the hillside to my right, I thought I saw some movement in the undergrowth. The hillside was covered with small silver birch saplings and I strained my eyes to see if the movement was in my imagination.

The sergeant's warnings were still fresh in my mind but I saw definite movement at the top of the hill. Having spent almost two hours without seeing a living person, it would be nice to find some farmer or similar, to pass the time of day with, I thought. I decided to walk up the hill towards the top where my view would be much better; in any case the sun had not yet reached the bottom of the valley and I could see its warming rays bathing the top of the hill. I had climbed half way up when my attention was again drawn to movement in the ferns a little higher up. I stopped in the thought that if it was a fox it would probably take flight. Not being a country person, I was not about to disturb some creature which I ignorantly thought could do me injury if caught by surprise. I then saw two distinct movements from the undergrowth about five yards apart. I walked slowly closer, being careful not to make too much noise. My quarry moved again and I could clearly make out now the shape of what looked like two people, crouching down in the undergrowth.

I was not keen to move closer without drawing attention to my presence. We all know how much of a shock it is when someone surprises us when we are concentrating on our task! I shouted "Hello", which seems stupid now but at the time was the only thing to come into my head. The two had clearly been watching my progress up the hill and immediately stood up. Both were dressed in strong outdoor clothing complete with cloth caps and heavy boots. One was holding what seemed to be a shotgun and the other a net. The one with the net had a two dogs by his side, a lurcher and a small terrier type.

To anyone reading this, the facts will seem straightforward, two poachers are caught red-handed by a policeman. It sounds funny now but I never saw it this way. I realised that they were taking some kind of game but this was common in the area. Many people were asked by farmers to go onto land and catch as many rabbits as possible to keep their numbers down. I was about to have a chat with them, totally dismissing any thought in my mind that they might have crouched down in an attempt to hide from me, when, before I could say anything, the nearest one blurted out,

"OK, we give ourselves up; you've caught us." The words did not sink in for a few seconds as they both moved towards me. I did not understand at this stage what on earth they were giving themselves up for! Two dead rabbits were handed to me, together with the net and a pheasant. The dogs were placed on leads. I thought to myself that if it was necessary for me to have the net and rabbits then I must surely have the shotgun. My brain was now working overtime in an attempt to find out exactly what they had done wrong, but something told me to I needed to maintain the upper hand now.

"Pass the gun over," I said in a no-nonsense fashion. "Is it loaded?" I continued.

"No I just fired it", said one of them and then he continued, "We shouldn't have gone out of the first field where we have got permission. We know its wrong but the rabbits seemed to be all in this area."

It seemed a little harsh to arrest them but trying to hide from me must count against them, I thought. Kidsgrove Police never arrested poachers, mainly because the poachers were too crafty for us, but here I was with the evidence straight out of a training centre question paper. This was my hour of glory and I decided I was going to take it with both hands.

"Right you two, you are both under arrest for poaching and I must warn you that anything you say, etc........."

We all walked back to the road and set off towards the police station. By now I had even taken charge of the two dogs who were pulling me along quite oblivious to the difficulties their owners were in. It was nearly 9am as we neared the station, passing the occasional local who just stopped and stared at us. We must have looked a pretty unusual site, rarely seen in the centre of the town.

As we climbed the station steps, my enthusiasm was suddenly dulled somewhat by the face of Sergeant Hancock at the window. His expression was not one of delight! Indeed as I entered the office and started relating the circumstances to the office constable, he just slipped his coat on and went home for his breakfast.

"You deal with it Arthur, I will be back at ten after I have eaten." Arthur grinned at me in a knowing sort of way as the Sergeant vanished. Don't worry," he said, "I will sort out some charges for you."

Arthur then rang the local butcher with a request to store the dead animals in his deep freeze until wanted for Court. The gun and net were placed in the miscellaneous property store and labelled. The dogs were thought to be too much of a problem for us to cope with and were handed back!

Two weeks later a serious looking bunch of magistrates thanked me for bringing these criminals before them, before handing out some hefty fines. I was eventually forgiven by the Sergeant but the general consensus was reached that they should not send me out of the town centre in future!

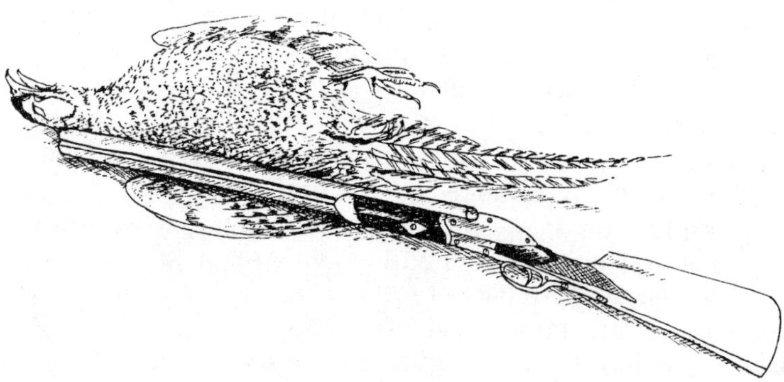

"RAG BONE, RAG BONE"

The rag and bone man with his faithful horse and cart had become extinct in most areas of the Country by the time I started foot patrol. Certainly in my home town of Stafford, the plaintive cry of "Rag, bone; any old rag bone?" was a thing of the past. I certainly had never before seen a horse and cart going around the streets collecting all manner of old metal from bikes to worn out dolly tubs. These were the 1960's and if anyone in Stafford was to start up in business collecting old metal, he would certainly not use a horse and cart. I may have seen the odd scrap metal lorry touring the streets, with its driver touting for old car batteries but even instances of this sort were few and far between in Stafford.

The Steptoe and Son days were numbered, or so I thought until I started exploring Kidsgrove, where I began to see quite a few horses and carts touring the streets and I often wondered where on earth they all appeared from. The horses were sometimes found wandering the streets in the middle of the night, having escaped from their tether in a bid to find some lush roadside grass verge. The sparks from their shoes scraping on the blue bricks of the footpaths as they raced to avoid capture in the dead of night, was a spectacle to be seen! It took some time for me to locate where they were all appearing from and this again was also a sight to behold - a wagon train of carts emerging from a gateway at the top of Kidsgrove Bank at around 8.30am every day! Some turned right and headed for the City area and a few turned left down to Kidsgrove and the surrounding villages. Some, occasionally, even ventured up to Harriseahead and Mow Cop! The steepness of some of the climbs made me wonder how on earth the horses managed to keep their footing. A few balloons or a goldfish changed hands for a bag of old clothes or a pram with only two wheels. You may laugh, but a pram with all of its wheels would never be parted with because with a few simple design changes, it became a de-luxe go-cart. Every street at that time had about half a dozen of these contraptions which had no means of propulsion other than gravity. They were easy to get started on a downhill bit of road and easy to steer using a piece of string tied around each side of the front axle, but they were damned difficult to stop! Apart from dragging your feet along the ground, the only other sure way of stopping was to hit something fairly substantial like a wall!

Although the rag and bone carts, complete with their fit looking horses, could travel many miles each day, it was unusual for them to climb back out of Kidsgrove to Talke Pits. The hill taking the shortest route to the village was just too much, even for the toughest Tunstall mount. The only way for them into the village was by going the long way round and crossing the main A34 trunk road. The carts held their own in traffic and were rarely involved in accidents; after all, if you were one of the lucky ones in your street to own a car then the last thing in the world you wanted was to hit a cart made 30 years ago to plans that would have done Noah's Ark proud - and even if you could prove that it was the cart owner's fault, would you expect him to produce a crisp certificate of insurance for you to claim on? But although usually heavily tatooed and looking like something out of a Charles Dickens story, they were no more dangerous than any other member of the community and to be fair, they were mainly law abiding people, just trying to make an honest bob or two.

I had been called to a house, again in my happy hunting ground of Queen Street, Talke Pits, to a report of stealing. The houses were in a long terrace block with entries at intervals giving access to the rear gardens. Some will remember with nostalgia the outside loo with torn up newspaper on a hook behind the door. It must have been quite hygienic to have all of those horrible smells out in the garden, not inside the house. After all there were no 'Haze Spring Fresh' sprays in those days! Outside loos were the thing for Queen Street. On very cold nights when the frosts were cold enough to burst the pipes, the smell of pink paraffin lingered in the air. The paraffin lamp was trimmed and it filled the loo with a warm looking glow through the glass cover. How such a small lamp could fight against a gale blowing through huge gaps at the top and bottom of the door defied belief, but the pipes didn't seem to suffer as long as one was kept lit. Each house had its own toilet with a massive wooden seat and it was strategically placed right at the bottom of the garden.

I arrived at the house where the theft had taken place, to be greeted by an old lady somewhere in her 70's. She was clearly very upset as she described to me how she had returned home from the corner shop to discover that the lead from the roof of her toilet was missing. I found it hard not to smile as she described how her husband had retired to the bottom of the garden for what she described as "a quiet half an hour". I was not sure whether he had a medical complaint to cause him to be closeted away for so long but now was not the time to discuss it. As we walked towards the structure in question, she described how a sudden heavy burst of rain had driven her husband back into the house. Quite clearly, the lead had performed a very useful purpose during the last 30 years, but not any more. It had been stripped from the roof and was no doubt now in some scrapyard, totally unrecognisable, I thought.

I took down a short statement; this always gives some comfort to an injured party and to show that I was trying to solve the crime, I went knocking on doors in the street. People are more likely to help in an enquiry such as this if they think it could happen to them next, so at each house I asked to see if their lavatory roof was still intact and loaned my torch for them to check. When it was established that they had not been victims, I asked if they had noticed any strangers in the area.

I had drawn a blank with my enquiries and was about to give up for the night when a neighbour said, "The only stranger in the street today was a rag and bone man." This could be just the break I needed to stop a 'flood' of similar thefts in the area. After all, if he got away with one lavatory roof, what was to stop him clearing the street?

"Can you remember what he looked like?" I asked, "or what he was wearing?"

"Sorry, officer. I didn't take much notice of him. I didn't know he was going to take the lead from the roof, did I?"

It was proving hard work, and I thought I was going to have difficulty getting even the basic details from her, when she gave me just the information I needed.

"He had a horse and cart with him. The cart was at the bottom of the street," she said. I pumped her for more information and received the unexpected statement, "I would recognise his horse if I saw it again!"

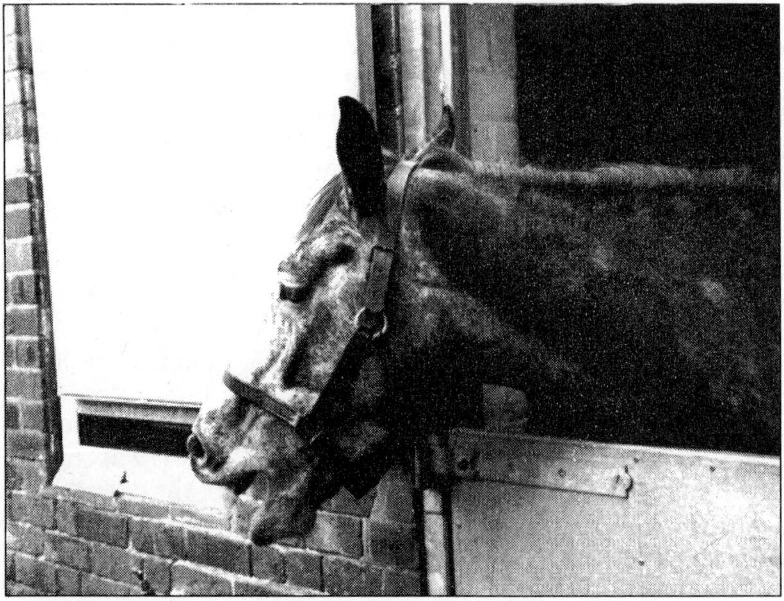

It was too late that night to go hunting the streets for a particular coloured horse and I said that I would call round to collect her the following afternoon at 3pm. She was waiting in the street as I arrived in an ex-GPO Mini van. She climbed in and within a few minutes we were parked outside the entrance to the scrapyard which was home to the horse and cart brigade. We waited until 3.45pm at which time there began a steady stream of carts returning to the yard.

She seemed fairly confident as each cart went by. "No that's not the one," she assured me. Suddenly as one rounded the corner, she said, "That's the horse that was in our street yesterday."

Although we had all learnt how to caution offenders at the training centre, this was real life! No such thing as solicitors, especially for the likes of him. I climbed out of the van leaving the lady safely behind and signalled the driver of the cart to stop as I walked over to him.

"Jump down; you are in big trouble mate," I said.

"Why, what's up?" he replied.

"Don't mess me about. You were in Queen Street yesterday and the lead went off the lavatory roof of one of the houses - and I can prove it was you; you're under arrest!" He seemed to easily accept the fact that he was being denied his liberty - always a good sign. He had not admitted anything at this stage, so he needed to see the friendly side of me just yet!

"If you are reasonable, you can go and see to the horse before we go to the station. If not; you can leave it where it is and hope nobody takes it." He didn't mind being locked up but the thought of losing his horse was enough to tip the balance.

"Alright. It's true; I took the lead. Just one thing, how did you find out it was me?" he asked.

"Your horse is an unusual colour and the locals took note of it," I answered.

"Well I'll be damned! I never thought I would be caught because of the old horse," he said. I walked to a telephone box and within minutes the rag bone man was 'carted' off to the station in the police car. I took one very satisfied lady home and the lead was recovered from the yard. I don't know if the old boy had any luck rolling it back on the roof but the crime of the week had been solved using house to house enquiries together with more than a certain amount of luck!

TAKING WILD BIRDS

Dabba was a likeable rogue in his early thirties who lived with his mother in Queen Street, Talke Pits. He walked to work across the scrub land near to his home and remained throughout the day on what can only be described as a rubbish tip.

The land was 'owned' by the local farmer who took me into his confidence; so much so that I used to borrow his motor mower and use his holiday caravan. The land in question could only be described as scrub land which had never been cultivated. It had a steep drop at the edge, the importance of which was not valued until much later when land fill sites were in demand. The farmer had confided to me that the Council had tried to claim the land as theirs, but due to a lack of documentary evidence, they could not prove it conclusively. He had moved into a large rambling house in the village many years before and he had adopted the land as his own at that time. His argument was quite clear. "They say it's theirs and I say it's mine. I haven't got any papers to prove it and neither have they! The difference is, I have put a fence round it; so I will win in the end!" He turned out to be right; the Council finally gave up trying to claim it and the farmer wasted no time in having a solicitor register it in his name.

Part of the land was then sold to Walkers Century Oils where a large factory making hand cleaning liquid was built. On the part near to the tip stood a motley collection of large sheds of the type left over after the War. These were occupied by a small company called Talke Paints. No paint was ever made there; no plant existed even, to make it. It was just a row of sheds, one of which had a telephone in it. The owner was a man in his 30's who employed Dabba on a daily basis. The main way paint found its way to the 'factory' was when a large engineering firm wanted to dispose of gallons of faulty paint and they rang Talke Paints. Thus most of the paint was bright yellow! The firm did have some green paint at one time and I clearly remember using some of it to paint my kitchen doors. The only problem was the paint never dried! In hindsight, we should have sold it as anti-burglar paint for drain pipes! But then we would have been 20 years ahead of our time!

My connection with the company was simple; I worked for them in the afternoon, answering the telephone or loading fifty gallon drums onto lorries. When the boss and Dabba went out in the transit van, I was left to man the phone. The pay was about £3 for an afternoon which was most welcome. A bonus was to get oil for my mini van and in any case I was out in the fresh air - usually wearing an old shirt and ripped jeans. Any visitors had no idea of my official identity and so it usefully brought me into contact with a number of villains!

Dabba was a bit unsure at first of whether he could trust me and even then he only 'allowed' me information which he was confident could not be traced back to him. I knew that my working arrangement was safe because the Inspector was a good friend of the owner of Talke Paints and I was aware that from time to time, he 'borrowed' the firm's van. He knew what I was up to and I knew what he was up to! On one occasion the owner confided to me that the Inspector had been travelling up the M1 when the sliding door fell off - I would dearly have loved to hear his explanation to the motorway police!

There was another rather different small business some 150 yards from the paint factory, tucked away in a small coppice of trees. Although the paint factory occasionally suffered at the hands of burglars, no doubt due to its isolated position, this other business had no such problems; they bred Staffordshire bull terriers, a type of dog which is soft enough with people but becomes fighting mad when they come across other dogs. If ever two of the dogs managed to get within biting distance of one another, all hell was let loose. The dogs had huge jaws which locked into place around their opponent's neck and they hung on despite anything anyone could do to the dog's rear end! You could hit it with a stick but it just stayed put, biting even harder. When alone, the dogs were very friendly and liked to play - it was as if there was a switch on their backs, with a nasty and nice programme. The wire runs were left untouched by passing vandals - a very wise decision; who says vandals are all stupid!

One of the tasks we undertook at the paint factory was to make a special grease for use in the coal mines. The contract was from the National Coal Board and had been awarded to Walker's Century Oils, to provide the thick grease to lubricate the wheels of coal trucks and conveyor belts in the pits. For some time, Walker's mixed the grease at their Hanley depot until one day the process started a serious fire in the centre of Hanley. It was decided that the process would have to be moved well away from any type of habitation. The paint factory was just what they wanted and so the owner was given instructions on exactly how to mix the evil brew. The three of us set up a huge metal tank, square in shape with a round hole at the top measuring about 2 feet across. The tank was placed on two huge mounds of earth leaving a space beneath where we could light a fire. I think you will understand the reluctance of Walkers to perform this operation when I tell you what was put into the tank. First we broke up large bags of solidified bitumen; that is the stuff used to make flat roofs watertight and which looks like shiny black liquorice when it splits. The process then required us to light a huge fire beneath the tank and wait for the bitumen to melt. We then added some other substances which I am unable to remember, followed by - I know you won't believe it - benzene! Yes, you are right; benzene is very inflammable which made the task dodgy to say the least, but if I tell you that we poured it from 45 gallon drums into the top of the tank, you would be right to call us crazy. One slip and the benzene would go up in flames. We then took a huge paddle and stirred the mixture for about an hour until it was ready to be drained off into 5 gallon drums.

I never had any problems myself, but poor old Dabba was mixing on his own one day when I was on police duty. I saw the fire engine heading towards the paint factory and guessed immediately what had happened. Dabba had serious burns to his hands and arms and I found it difficult when I visited him later, in my official role of constabulary, to ask him what had caused the fire, when both of us knew full well what he had been doing!

His boss visited him, both at hospital and when he came home, and he provided his wages during his recuperation. In those days it was most unusual for an employer to go out of his way like this, but we all knew that our little earner was finished if too many enquiries were made by the Council.

I can picture Dabba now, a huge overweight man, lying in bed with his arms swathed in massive bandages; the boss was giving his mother flowers and assuring her that his money would continue until he was back at work, and I sat there in my uniform trying to make conversation - we must have looked an unusual trio.

For all his faults, Dabba and I had a soft spot for each other, although he otherwise disliked police officers and eyed them all with great suspicion. Perhaps he felt that I was much too young to have real authority and therefore I was not a threat to his sidelines. To tell the truth, even the Council could not believe that there wasn't a person of voting age in charge of the police station; so much so that when I sent back the official voting form indicating that we were all under 21 years of age, they sent it back to Kidsgrove with a sarcastic note attached, requesting that the correct details be inserted!

On another part of the land there lived an elderly man and his permanently intoxicated wife. The caravan they lived in was kept very neat and tidy mainly due to the fact that the husband kept out of his wife's way; he could be found in his engineering shed at all hours of the day and night. He befriended me and when I started to moan about the high price of electricity he offered to slow down my meter for me. He was not joking and he showed me the seals and the equipment required to put the meter back after the inside had been 'fixed'. I declined the offer - my job would certainly vanish if they found out my meter was only recording half the electricity being delivered!

The tip and the scrub land was central in position to the Walker's factory, the caravan and the paint factory. One day, Dabba gave me a tip that there were men wandering onto the land and that they were up to no good. Dabba did not elaborate when I first questioned it and I left him to stew for a few weeks until he was glad to get it off his chest. While he would not split on local yobs who took cars or broke into the local corner shop, he loved animals and did not like to see them hurt. We were having a cup of tea on a lovely summer's afternoon at the paint factory when he decided to tell me all he knew about the goings on in the fields nearby.

"I think they are catching birds, you know," he said.

"What makes you think that Dabba?" I replied.

"Its just the way the two blokes have been walking across the fields and then vanishing for a couple of hours before walking back to the village. They are locals - they must be up to no good. Why would anyone stay down there for so long if they weren't up to something? I reckon they are after the birds." Being from the town, I had not heard of this one before and I tried to quiz him for more information.

"If they catch birds, what do they do with them? They're too small to eat, Dabba," I said.

"They sell them, don't they; finches and the like cost quite a bit of money. They put rings on them and say they've bred them at home. Once they are in a cage, it is hard to tell a wild one from one bred at home. It's easy money for them but its cruel and I don't like it going on round here."

Dabba said this with a hint of revenge in his voice. When we parted company that day, I said, "If you see them in the fields Dabba, just give me a ring and I will come down and see what they are up to."

About a week later, just as I was about to eat my lunch the telephone rang. "Its Dabba," the voice said, "if you come down now you'll catch them. But remember not to tell who put you onto them."

I rushed to pull my uniform trousers on and look like a policeman - the uniform was my insurance against getting beaten up miles from anywhere. The police uniform generated great respect and I thought, if people visiting the station ask to see my Dad when I'm out of uniform, then poachers were hardly likely to do as I asked. My lunch was left on the table - I knew Dabba would be checking my reaction time; he would not trust me with information next time if I failed to come up with the goods now.

I ran down the hill from the station into the lane and walked slowly along the hedge side looking hard to see what was going on in the fields almost half a mile away. The good thing was, if I could not see them, then, they could not see me. I carried my helmet under my arm and decided to increase my speed until I was on open ground. I then stopped to survey the fields which were a series of mounds and hollows. It was rather like looking out from a small boat at huge rolling waves. One minute you were on the top of a mound and the prey was in a hollow - only when both were on the crest of a wave could you see one another. I caught a glimpse of one man who appeared to be holding a branch broken from a tree.

When I had got to within 100 yards, I moved very slowly and carefully, hardly making a sound. I watched the two men from a distance for about ten minutes during which time nothing much happened. I was soon getting bored watching men sitting on the grass apparently just sunbathing so I decided to get closer.

For a short while I was not seen and then to my horror one of the men stood up and looked directly at me. I was unsure whether he had seen that I represented the law and I stood up, put my helmet on and ran at full speed towards them. I was sure that they would run like hell also and I had decided to select just one to go for and hope that he was the slowest.

I started to shout at the top of my voice, "Stop you are under arrest, it's the police." Normally this had the effect of making the fugitive go even faster as the adrenalin flowed - the effect it had on me was to make me even more breathless!

To my surprise, the men looked towards me and stayed transfixed to the spot. They did not even raise a fast walk, which surely would have ensured that one at least would escape. It was a complete mystery to me why they were giving in so easily; perhaps Dabba had been wrong and they were indeed just sun bathing? What on earth was I arresting them for in that case? I took the last few yards at a more leisurely pace, which enabled me to appear more dignified than a few minutes before when I had resembled a red indian about to take a scalp!

But soon my troubles were all over; there in the grass I saw the small wire cage used to place the call bird in. The idea was to leave a captured bird to give out distress calls. Birds of the same type would be attracted to the call and land on a conveniently placed branch which had been covered in what is known as bird lime. This is a thick glue from which the unfortunate bird cannot escape. He then calls in distress himself attracting others. All the system required was one bird, a cage and patience. My little poachers had all the equipment including a jar of bird lime, the small wire cage with the call bird and some recently taken finches to boot. I made the usual pronouncement to them, "You are both under arrest for taking wild birds. You do not have to say anything, etc, ...," after which I led them back across the fields.

I was puzzled as to why they had not taken to their heels and made a run for it when they had first seen me. As we set off, I could see that one of them was walking a little stiffly but I did not think much about it at first as we were in no real hurry.

"Most people try and run away from the police," I said casually. "No doubt you realised that I am very fit and decided against it."

"There wouldn't be much point in me running," said one of them, lifting his trouser leg. "You can't run with a leg like this," he said pointing out a polished round piece of what looked like mahogany. Sure enough he had a full wooden leg complete with a rubber tip on the end!

We were provided with transport to Kidsgrove where I felt it prudent not to mention the man's incapacity. The two waited in the cells while law books were produced and searched for various offences. We started with the law about confining a bird in a cage in which it could not stretch its wings, but then decided to call in the experts from the RSPCA who would know how to throw the book at them.

It was the first case of its kind ever at Kidsgrove and it caused a great deal of interest in the local press. And Dabba was now my trusted friend who regularly updated me with goings-on in the village. My reputation for seeking out unusual offences thus continued to grow by the day!

YOU CAN'T PARK HERE, SIR!

One of the skills I learnt at the Training Centre in early 1966 was the art of directing traffic - traffic signals. Out on the parade ground we were assembled into classes of about 20 constables, given the military term of 'squads' and we were marched around to the bellowed orders of "Squad, shun!" which roughly translated means, 'everyone stand to attention'. Music would then blare out from loud speakers and we performed arm signals in time with the music. Passing lorry drivers would toot their horns in amusement at the sight of hundreds of uniformed police officers waving their arms about to direct imaginary traffic!

At this time, traffic problems were high on the agenda of our tasks; although cars were not owned by the vast majority of people, there were enough about to cause problems for the police and then, houses had not been built with the car in mind; garages and drives were few and far between which meant that out of necessity, many vehicles were parked in the road. Yellow lines had not been introduced yet into town centres and the existing laws were derived from the horse and cart era. 'Obstructing the highway' was the way matters were described to us and I recall the training officer telling us "the roads are for driving vehicles along and not a huge car park. If you cannot drive along the road because of parked cars, then the owners should be dealt with using the full force of the law!"

I am reminded of this each time my wife wants to use her car now and insists that I move mine from the drive so that she can leave. I could be lazy and leave it on the road outside but I still regard it as an offence. Clearly with the passage of time attitudes have changed and as a result the roads are clogged with abandoned vehicles. I can understand the unfortunate individual who has no drive and lives in a row of terraced houses; he has no option but to use the road as a car park. But I have no sympathy with the selfish individual who causes other drivers to weave continually in and out of parked cars when he has somewhere else to put it.

Clearly present day officers do not look upon the problem as being worth bothering about. In the street where I live, we have an inspector and a constable who regularly cause difficulties for other residents by cluttering the road with their vehicles. Following a series of complaints to headquarters about the problem, the excuse was that he could not afford six paving slabs to extend the parking area in front of his bungalow. I smiled when extensions to his property costing thousands of pounds were embarked upon a few months later.

He was fortunate not to have lived in Kidsgrove on any of the routes I patrolled as a probationary constable! One day Jim Murphy, a senior constable, was called into the office to join me and the Inspector, to discuss a problem with car parking at ICL (International Computers Limited) on the outskirts of Butt Lane. The Inspector had received a complaint from the Council regarding the haphazard parking outside the factory and we were to monitor the situation over a period of days.

The factory was not on my area and so I had little idea of what to expect. Another factor in the equation which was of utmost importance was that in those days a small police station such as Kidsgrove needed to retain close links with the owners of large businesses on a 'you scratch my back and I'll scratch yours' basis. There was nothing really corrupt about this, but it did mean that the Christmas party for the police children could take place without charge, in the large dining hall of ICL. There was a similar practice at our parent station, Newcastle, who used Rists Wires and Cables as their benefactor; and Traffic Group used the main G.E.C. factory at Stafford for their events. The companies were only too pleased to help the local constabulary, who by comparison to industry were poorly paid and needed all the help they could get. The companies involved did not seek any special favours in return but when the telephone rang at the crack of dawn with an urgent request to move a 600 ton generator to the Cheshire border, you can be sure it was all hands to the pumps - the paperwork was delivered by motorcycle outriders who looked like they were in the Isle of Man T.T. races. It was just our little way of saying thank you!

With the childrens' Christmas party in mind on the one

side and the pressure from the local Council on the other, this parking matter would need very careful and sensitive handling. The Inspector insisted that nothing was to be done until an appraisal of the situation was concluded. Jim and I set off on foot to see how serious the problem was. The factory was almost new and had been designed with the car in mind; the main buildings were set back from the road with huge car parks provided at the back of the buildings. The car parks were clearly signed and colour coded, with red, blue, yellow and green signs. If you worked in one section near to the Butt Lane end then you were asked to use the red park at the rear of your building. Nothing could have been simpler for all concerned. There had been no cases of vandalism to cars using the car parks or any other obvious reasons not to use the facility. The buildings were on both sides of the road and were modern with large picture windows. We could see the workers moving about in the offices on the second floor, using drawing boards and such like to design the newly introduced computers we had heard so much about. Unfortunately our police technology at the time was restricted to a biro! There were small brick security lodges at each entrance which had 24 hour cover by uniformed guards.

As we walked along the road the problem became evident - a long string of cars parked bumper to bumper as far as the eye could see - and they were parked on both side of the road, not just one! The effect was to reduce the width of the road to such an extent that two cars travelling in opposite directions had to slow to a crawl to ensure they did not collide. Whenever a lorry making a delivery came along, there was a great deal of manouevring and reversing.

We decided to visit the security lodge and we introduced ourselves to the smartly dressed guard inside. The reason for our visit was explained and without further discussion he made a telephone call to the personnel department. Within a few minutes we were invited up to the rather grand offices and made welcome with a cup of coffee. The situation was explained as well as the fact that the Council had expressed concern about it - it was always best to try to lay the blame for any action firmly on the shoulders of a third party - we then became the referee in the situation and the anger could be deflected from ourselves, the friendly local police.

We all gazed through the window and agreed that the parking was out of hand. We explained that our wish was to deal with the matter with kid gloves, which prompted the management to offer a solution. Clearly all of the vehicles were owned by employees of the company although no explanation was offered for why the car parks were unused. Posters, they suggested, would be produced by ICL and displayed in all the offices and even in the canteen. It was agreed that this was a good form of action and would probably produce the desired effect.

For several days we continued to monitor the situation, reporting back our findings to the Inspector. He agreed that the signs would probably resolve the situation without any blood having to be spilt, and indeed, some staff did heed the request, reducing the number of cars left on the road but not sufficiently to please the Council. Unfortunately, the die-hards continued to park on the road, unconcerned by our regular visits.

We remained puzzled at the reluctance of the drivers to use the parks provided, until one afternoon we stayed later. The second the clock hit 5pm, the rush of people from the factory was something to behold. Streams of people hurried out of the gates towards their vehicles, starting their engines as if their lives depended upon it and pulling away like a Le Mans start. Those parked in the road were first away to join the queue at the traffic lights; the good citizens who had obeyed the request to use the designated car parks struggled to join the queue in the main road and were destined to wait up to ten minutes for their turn to start the run for home. It certainly threw a new light on the situation and we were especially concerned that the law abiding were being penalised for their trouble.

The whole situation was recorded in my report which concluded that no amount of persuasion was going to influence the law breakers; action was needed at the earliest opportunity! The company had done everything in its power to help us and they agreed that nothing more could be done on their side. Indeed the numbers of cars left on the road was gradually increasing again as workers saw the futility of complying with our request. At least we had tried the pleasant way of dealing with the matter; it was now time to show our teeth!

The Inspector had a cunning plan! In order to obtain clear evidence that the road was obstructed by parked vehicles, he intended to involve the Council. A letter was written outlining the situation and requesting that the mechanical road sweeper be designated to sweep the road outside the factory. If it was unable to sweep the gutters, then, he argued, this would be clear evidence that the parked vehicles were causing an unneccessary obstruction.

The following Monday, Constable Murphy walked with me to the factory where we were met by the Inspector. The mechanical sweeper arrived at 9am and made its futile way down the road and then back again. For the whole length of the road, its brushes never reached closer than five feet from the gutter, making two wet marks on the middle of the road but little else. Leaves and general debris remained stubbornly in the gutter and to our amusement, the council worker offered to use a hand brush to clean around the parked cars! Obviously his bosses had not enlightened him of the situation. A statement was obtained from him outlining that, due to the parked cars, he had been unable to sweep the road.

We now needed evidence that the cars parked at 9am were in the same place at 3pm, thus showing that the unnecessary obstruction was for a reasonable period. Constable Murphy started at one end of the road and I started at the other, writing down the registration numbers and the type of vehicle in our pocket books. We met in the middle some fifteen minutes later. Although the staff in the offices had been used to seeing us patrol the road regularly in the past two weeks, the sight of us recording the registration numbers caused not a little concern, and one or two came into the road and removed their cars to the car park.

We had our lunch and on the dot of 3pm we started once again to move down the row of cars, but this time leaving a form HORT.1 on each windscreen, beneath the wiper blade. There were no yellow lines or fixed penalty notices in those days; indeed no forms even to deal with this type of incident. Jim and I took it upon ourselves to leave the form normally used to give personally to a motorist following a verbal request to take his documents to a police station of his choice. A copy of the form was sent back to the station indicated, if after waiting two weeks nothing had been heard. The form was not a requirement in law, just a reminder to the person to take his documents within 5 days to the station. The form was taken from him and sent with the document details to the officer who had issued it. If this sounds complicated, it actually wasn't in practice!

We filled in the details of the vehicle on one side of the form and on the other we wrote a polite note - "Please visit Kidsgrove Police Station within 5 days." Fixed penalty notices are all that is needed nowadays but in the 60s a constable must see you personally - and point out to you the offence committed. You were then cautioned - "You do not have to say anything unless, etc,........ " and finally you were told that the facts would be reported - you could not then say that you were unaware of what you had done. Our problem was that each of the 100 drivers must now be seen and reported for the offence of obstructing the highway. Our plan was to start off an offence book for each car and the full details could be filled in when the driver came to the police station.

It was not long before word spread around the factory that the police were leaving some kind of notice on the cars parked along the road. Some ignored it but others scuttled out in a vain attempt to move the cars. We had spent too much time on the problem now and after all, they had declined to move them when requested; this was our day and none were to escape. The drivers plucked the forms HORT.1 from their windscreens and read them.

"Can't we see you now, came the request from several drivers."

"Afraid not; please take your insurance and licence to Kidsgrove. We've got to finish handing out the rest of the forms," I said.

It took us some time to put forms on all of the cars but by 4.15pm the job was finished. We were not popular with the ICL workers at this stage but we were even more unpopular with the station constable at Kidsgrove. It took us some time to walk back to the station, giving many of the erring motorists a head start. By the time we approached the steps to the station, we could see, standing outside, quite a queue of disgruntled drivers waiting to be dealt with. Some must have carried their documents with them and others had been home to collect them. Although they had some idea that by parking on the road they had caused annoyance, they were not prepared for the fact that the police were taking them to Court for it. For several hours we all helped record the details as they continued to drift in to find out what the notes meant.

The pile of completed offence books grew and the instructions to us were that, when they were all finished they would be dealt with all together in one Court sitting. After the five days had elapsed, just one book was outstanding, which was unfortunately one which I had issued. It was not a bad tally from a total of 100, but none the less the others could not go in without it. I rang the local car tax office in Stafford who told me that the documents were with the Cheshire Tax Office. A phone call to them gave me the owners details; he lived in Congleton, Cheshire, which tied in with the location of the factory; many workers at ICL came from the leafy areas of Cheshire.

It happened to be my weekend off and, in any case, I would need permission to take the police car into another area to visit the man, so I took it upon myself to go the following day in my own car - I took the offence book with me and drove to Congleton in my own time; it seemed a natural thing to do at the time, but on reflection it was a mistake. I searched around the uncharted streets looking for his address - in normal circumstances it would be easy enough to stop and ask directions, but not in police uniform! Eventually I found his home, a comfortable semi-detached on a little estate. The car was not outside and I had a premonition that my journey had been wasted as I knocked on the door. There was no reply and again no sign of life when I went to the back door and I returned to my car to think things over. I should have anticipated this problem, but it had never crossed my mind. The last thing I wanted to do now was to have to return to Congleton a second time. I would put a note through his door, I decided, asking him again to come to Kidsgrove Police Station. The only paper I had, apart from my pocket book, was a form HORT.1. It did not occur to me that I was using the same form with the same request on the back, that I had used already to no avail! The form was scribbled out and pushed through the letter box and I gave a sigh of relief and drove home. My conscience felt clear; I had given it my best shot; whatever happened now was out of my control.

The driver obviously got the message and visited Kidsgrove Station a few days later to report to the office constable. A note was attached to the book stating that he would plead 'not guilty' to the charge. Never mind, I thought as I handed the completed books in; I had done as I was told and everyone had been dealt with correctly and efficiently. Within two weeks I received a notice requiring me to give evidence at the Magistrates Court. The ninety-nine cases were dealt with in quick time by the magistrates who warned each driver of the consequences if the offence was repeated. "The police will visit again and if any cars are in the road, the fines will not be nearly so lenient," said the presiding lady magistrate, imposing a £5 fine on each offender.

Finally the offender from Congleton appeared in Court to plead "not guilty", in a clear voice. Gradually it began to dawn on me that he was not just a run of the mill driver; in fact it turned out that he was a retired Cheshire police officer. The facts were read out by the Inspector who indicated that the driver was the only one to fail to call at Kidsgrove when requested the first time. The offender explained this by saying the note must have fallen off in the wind. A plausible explanation I thought, but highly unlikely when ninety-nine others remained attached to the windscreens! Each item of evidence was challenged and the magistrates seemed anxious to listen to his various arguments concerning the law in use. Eventually it was my turn in the witness box. My hands were clammy with sweat as I started my evidence.

"Police Constable number 104, Trevor Houlton, stationed at Talke Pits; your worships. At 9am on......."

The easy part was to describe the road full of cars preventing the sweeper doing its job, but the defendant was not really interested in challenging me on this. He waited until I said, "Each car number was recorded and I put a note under the windscreen wiper asking the driver to call at Kidsgrove Police Station."

"Did all 100 visit the station, Constable?" he asked.

"No, one did not, which caused us a slight delay," I replied. He then asked me a question which hit me below the belt.

"Was it you who came to my house and pushed this scruffy piece of paper through my door?"

He held the note out. He had ambushed me. I had to tell the truth and as I took hold of what was indeed a scruffy piece of paper, my heart began to pound. The cat was out of the bag; everyone, including my own Inspector would now hear how I drove into another police area in full uniform and conducted enquiries without permission. I could see at a glance that it was indeed my writing on the back of the form HORT.1.

"Yes, I did drive to your house when no one came to Kidsgrove to be reported," I said.

He continued, "Don't you think it is a little unprofessional to push scraps of paper through peoples' letterboxes?"

I knew that what I had done was not an ideal way of dealing with it but what else could I have done in the situation; after all, it was his fault that I needed to go to his house in the first place. If he had been reasonable, like the others, then the situation would never have arisen. I was beginning to wish the ground would open up and swallow me. Could I plead the 5th Amendment as they do in America?

"I had no other paper with me and I........." It was at this stage that the magistrate intervened.

"Officer, just let me establish what you are trying to tell us. Is it true that you placed fifty notes on cars parked outside ICL requesting the drivers to call at Kidsgrove Police Station? Constable Murphy did the same with fifty more and as a result ninety-nine drivers did as requested?"

"Yes, your Worship, that is what happened," I replied.

She continued, "Because you were one book missing, you drove to Congleton in your own car, in uniform, on your day off?"

"Yes, your Worship," I replied, feeling myself getting hotter and hotter. The Inspector was looking towards the floor at this stage and was clearly displeased with how matters were going.

"You then found that the defendant was not at home and decided to push a note through his door?" the magistrate said.

The whole Court listened in stunned silence at this revelation and I could see that the Court Clerk, with his array of law books, was thinking of what, if any, rule I had broken.

"Yes, your Worships; that is my note," I said, handing it back to the defendant.

The three magistrates went into a huddle, whispering together for a few moments before the leader of the bench announced;

"We think that it is highly commendable that you take your duty so seriously, officer. To think that you went in your own time to Congleton in order to bring this man to justice is worthy of great praise. Inspector, please bring this to the attention of the Superintendent at Newcastle. This young officer is the type we need in Kidsgrove to get things done."

I felt so relieved, I wanted to jump out of the witness box but I managed to contain myself. The magistrate continued, "We find the defendant guilty of the charge of causing an unnecessary obstruction of the highway. He has caused a great deal of trouble for the officer dealing with the matter therefore we feel that the penalty should reflect this. He will be fined £10 which is double that imposed upon the others. Do not park there again or the fine will increase in proportion!"

I was unsure if this was a wise punishment but to my surprise, the defendant came straight over to me after the case and said, "Sorry officer; I know what it's like; I have been through it myself when I was in the force. You know how it is, it's always worth a try. No hard feelings I hope."

"No hard feelings at all," I replied, shaking his hand. After all, I had now got the full support of the Magistrates and even the Superintendent was to be told about me!

A CID FRIEND

I recall one really bad winter in about 1968 when the whole village was cut off from the rest of the world for weeks on end. Even the telephone lines were down, giving me freedom to work when I chose to. Ernest Talbot was a young constable in the CID who often came to my house with his young family to play cards. Stake money was one old penny but the interest it generated kept us up all hours of the night. Ernie was a particularly useful friend as he had the use of the CID van, and a recent innovation had equipped it with folding rear seats. This meant that it could carry four people or two people and a stray dog. During this spell of very bad weather, he suddenly appeared at my village police station having driven the long way round, through the City. He drank a cup of tea and then asked if I wanted to go for a drive in the snow. I was somewhat cautious and I showed him the memorandum from Headquarters which stated that police vehicles should not leave the main roads for any reason during the bad weather. He was quite unconcerned; quite the reverse he was keen to try out his rally driving skills in the van. Carried along by his enthusiasm, I put on my thick great coat and heavy boots ready for some fun; after all, who would know where we had been anyway?

I sat in the passenger seat and we left the village heading along the lane towards Halmerend. The snow was not too bad and the van was coping well with it despite having rear wheel drive. The lane was narrow with hedges on both sides and we admired the frost covered trees glinting in the weak winter sunshine. The wind had blown some of the snow through gaps in the hedge to form drift mounds along the road and as we approached these, Ernie accelerated each time and with the rear wheels spinning wildly we broke through them one at a time. On occasions it seemed that the van was grinding to a halt but Ernie urged me to bounce up and down in my seat to achieve more grip. He was clearly in his element locking the steering from side to side and bouncing off the snow covered embankments. I did not like to say anything but it seemed to me that the drifts were getting bigger the further we went down the lane; we must have covered well over two miles by now and I was a little concerned that climbing back up to Talke Pits might be a damn sight harder than it had been going down!

Eventually we ran into a very big drift and the wheels kept spinning to no effect. Ernie tried reversing and then going forwards again but the van refused to budge, so he decided more weight was required on the back wheels - and I was to be the weight! But when I came to get out my door would not open against the snow drift so I had to wind the window down and climb out of it onto the snow. I struggled to the back of the van, flung the doors open and with my feet on the tailgate and my hands gripping the roof, I jumped up and down for all I was worth. This had the desired effect as the wheels bit into the snow each time my full eleven stones went down. We eased through the drift but I looked over the roof of the van to see spreading away in front of us, yet more drifts even higher than any we had yet encountered. My worst fears had been realised and I began to regret ever leaving the village!

We stopped for a few minutes to discuss our predicament. What were we going to do to extricate ourselves from this situation? We decided that we could not retrace our steps because the lane was too narrow to turn round in; and the van was plainly not up to reverslng all the way back; we would just have to carry on no matter how high the drifts became! For several hours the process of me jumping up and down at the back of the van continued and it was dark before we eventually returned home. Fortunately no damage had been done - but I had learnt yet another valuable lesson the hard way!

At my village station, a kennel had been provided to accommodate stray dogs brought in by kind-hearted members of the public. Due to a lengthy period without use, I decided to use the kennel for my own purposes! I removed half of the sloping roof and placed hinges on it to allow access, made a small wooden ramp up to the entrance and put it at the very bottom of my garden. The inside was covered with straw and six point of lay hens, costing half a crown each, were introduced to their new home - scraps of food left by the children were re-cycled into lovely eggs! Problems only arose, of course, when official inspections were to take place or when some kind soul brought in a stray dog. On one such occasion, some local children arrived with what seemed a friendly mongrel and I fastened it to the drain pipe before ringing Ernie to help. If the dog could be conveyed to the Newcastle kennels that day my problem would be solved, and wasn't the CID van designed for just that purpose? Ernie obliged and duly arrived. We approached the dog, or should I say tried to, for it now proved that it was a Jekyll and Hyde character, snapping and snarling at anyone who went near it. My training had not included taming wild dogs and I could not understand how several small children had been able to tie string around its neck and lead him to the station in the first place. I had fastened the official police leather lead to his own collar to tie him up when he arrived; we now needed to untie him from the drainpipe and load him into the van.

We tried every method, even offering him biscuits but he was having none of it, bearing his teeth whenever we got within five yards of him. The yard brush was produced and used to pin him against the wall, whilst I tried to untie him. If Ernie made one little slip, my hands would feel the full brunt of his bite - by now he was biting great chunks out of the brush head! I was petrified and could only keep thinking of the risk the children must have taken to bring him in.

Eventually, I untied the lead and holding it at arms length, pulled the dog towards the van. He remained the most unfriendly dog I had seen for a long time and I was very keen to load him into the van quickly. I opened the driver's door and lifted him up onto the seat, closing the door quickly. The theory was that he would run to the back of the van and stay there until we reached the kennels at Newcastle. Ernie went round to the passenger side and with perfect timing opened the door. The dog leapt across to the passenger seat and with one bound was out through the door and scampering off down the hill towards the village. We could both be heard shouting things like, "Oh, what a naughty dog," as he vanished into the distance. The loss of the dog was not so hard to bear but the loss of the County dog lead would involve much tiresome paperwork! We searched in vain for the dog for some time, not contemplating how we would recapture him even if we found him because we were certainly not his favourite people!

We returned to the station and did what we always did in the police in such circumstances; we made a pot of tea. Hardly was the cup to my lips when a knock came at the door. The very same children had found our errant dog and he had come with them as good as gold back to the station.

The tea was forgotten as we told the children how he had escaped once and could they possibly put him in the back of our van?

"Course we can, Mister," the eldest said, and he lifted the dog on board.

"Its very kind of you," I replied, and the dog wagged his tail and ran around in the back of the van. We were very pleased to have him back and I was overjoyed that the lead was back in custody. The journey was uneventful, with the Newcastle police dog handler removing him at the other end. But the dog had a final surprise for us; when we set off to return, we found that the van had a certain strange smell about it. Two buckets full of disinfectant later, we were finally able to sit in the van, providing both windows were kept wide open!

Another story that involved my friend Ernie, happened one evening when the nights were drawing in and it was dark by 5pm. These short days are unpleasant for anyone but for shift workers they are particularly unpleasant since, when on night duty, you spend your whole time in perpetual darkness, sleeping during the few hours of daylight. It was about 7pm when the telephone rang at Kidsgrove station. Ernie was the duty CID officer but it would be true to say that only the more interesting calls would stir the CID into action! There was a shortage of manpower that evening, which had caused me to be diverted from Talke Pits to Kidsgrove. It had been something of a bonus because I was allowed to drive the new Panda car, so called because it had a light blue body and white doors. We were encouraged to drive it for a few miles and then park it in full view of the public. The flat cap which was worn whilst driving it would then be left inside the vehicle, being replaced by the traditional helmet. The theory behind this was simple; members of the public would see the car and subconsciously believe there was an officer nearby. Anyone seeing the self-same officer walking with his helmet some distance away, would think it was another officer! Like me, you are probably thinking, what a load of bull, but you must remember that this policy was decided after many high level meetings and must therefore have been correct!

I had been patrolling all areas of the town and had just arrived back at the station to complete some paperwork, when the office constable asked if I would man the phones whilst he visited the 'loo'. Although Ernie was only two doors away it would not have been protocol to ask the CID to carry out this task. A phone call came from a man who lived on a large council estate on the edge of the village of Talke Pits. He described to me how a few seconds earlier, he was watching TV with the curtains open and the light switched on, when he decided to close the curtains. As he went to the window which overlooked his back garden he was startled by the face of a man looking into his window. It annoyed me to realise that if I had been left alone to patrol my own village, I would have be within half a mile of the incident when it happened. What was worse, the station constable was still missing. I had no choice but to bang on Ernie's door. "Come and answer the phones for a few minutes," I pleaded, "There's a Peeping Tom in my village and I might catch him."

Ernie let the information slowly sink into his head and he was obviously thinking, as did most officers of a few years experience, that rushing about would not solve anything. Reluctantly, and only because he was a good mate of mine, he agreed to stand in for a few minutes. I raced out of the station to my Panda and with the wheels spinning, drove out of the yard on the five mile journey to the scene. I knew, in reality, that the offender could be several miles away by the time I arrived but at least the complainant would know we had tried our best. As is always the case, every set of traffic lights were against me! The panda had no siren or flashing blue light as it was only designed to get me from A to B in a faster time than it took to walk. My mind was racing, trying to out-think the offender and plan his route of escape. After all, he had been surprised and for a few minutes he would panic, possibly being forced to go by a route unfamiliar to him. I was thinking of all the alley ways and footpaths he could have taken as I pulled up outside the complainant's house.

Fortunately he had the presence of mind to be outside waiting for me and I beckoned him into the front passenger seat, pushing my brief case and paperwork onto the floor. As the door slammed shut, we pulled away and I said, "It's a long shot but I want to tour the area for a while in case you see him again. Do you think you would recognise him in the dark?"

My hopes rose when he said he was sure he could pick the man out. I drove slowly through the estate, gradually enlarging my search area, occasionally doubling back to retrace our path. There were few people on the streets, mainly children playing under the light of lamp posts. Other adults were mostly in pairs walking to the pub or corner shop. Our quarry would almost certainly be on his own and because of this he should stand out.

Time went by and although I was loathe to give up, I explained that after another fifteen minutes we would have to return to his home and complete a written statement. I had almost exhausted all of my ideas and the man was also at the stage of giving up, when I had a sudden inspiration; the estate was bordered on one side by the main village road and on the other side by the main A34 trunk road; a pathway led from the estate across some plots of land where self-build houses were being constructed, to a transport cafe on the opposite side of the A34. I said we would call it a day if this last sweep failed.

We drove through the village and joined the A34 at its junction with the newly built A500, turning left towards Talke. We climbed the hill towards the transport cafe which could be seen in the distance, dimly lit but silhouetted in the strong sodium lights of the main road. Call it providence or just good timing, but the figure of a man could be seen crossing the main road and as he walked across the cafe lorry park in the direction of a parked pantechnican, my friend, who had been silent for a while, suddenly shouted in my ear, "That's him over there." I entered the car park slowly, not wishing to startle the man by the presence of a police car and drove as close to him as I could without making it look obvious.

"Have a good look at him; are you sure he's the man?" I said.

"Yes, I am sure," came the firm reply.

By now the man was close to the pantechnican and was looking for his keys. I stopped the car and told my passenger not to move. I got out of the Panda and approached him.

"Can I have a word with you, please?" I enquired.

"Why, what's wrong officer?" he replied confidently. As soon as I was close enough to take hold of him without the chance of escape, I grabbed hold of his arm.

"You are under arrest. You have been seen and recognised as the man who was looking into the window of a house from the rear garden some 30 minutes ago." I was pleased with the reply I received,

"It was a mistake; I was looking for another address and got mixed up." This was just what I wanted; confirmation that he was indeed the man involved. His explanation could be examined very closely during interview but the matter of wrong identity had been ruled out!

My difficulty now was to get the prisoner back to Kidsgrove and into the cells. The witness would not take too kindly to having to sit in my car with him; but would Ernie come? He was my last resort. I had no need to worry; the radio call mentioning the word 'prisoner' brought him scurrying out of the station immediately - it is a word which seems to reach the part of a detective's brain that no other word can possibly hope to.

Back at the station, Ernie started questioning the man, while I obtained a witness statement from the complainant. Soon a statement under caution revealed the whole sorry episode. Our man was a long distance lorry driver who liked to look through windows in the hope of catching some young lady getting dressed. His occupation allowed him the free run of the country in order to indulge his pursuit. He said that he never let things get out of hand and he got his excitement from just looking. Perhaps we must remember that in those days there was only BBC to watch and adult movies on 'Sky' were a long way away. But then perhaps with time, he may have progressed with his fetish, who knows; but an appearance before the Magistrates certainly dampened his enthusiasm and the story received a great deal of coverage in our local press who sold it on to the press in his home town. The sheer humiliation no doubt taught him a lesson even without the bonus of a large fine from our magistrates.

I was just happy that my village could sleep easily again and I vowed to use every means at my disposal not to be drawn back to Kidsgrove too often again at the expense of my local customers!

BROKEN WINDOWS

It only takes a few seconds to break a window and make off without any clues, leaving a hapless constable to pick up the pieces. The paint factory at Talke Pits was a regular target for stone throwers and I had this under control by doing a deal with the culprits; I would not tell their parents as long as they paid for the damage from their weekly pocket money! These crimes were never recorded.

At one end of the Main Street in the village of Talke Pits, there was a small hardware shop, selling everything from mops to paraffin It was in the days of Esso Blue and I was a regular caller for a top up of my gallon can. The staff were two village ladies, who were both very helpful and obliging. Mrs Hancock was in charge and she knew me well because her husband was a police sergeant and later on, an inspector at Kidsgrove. He was a tall, well-built man, always fair and straightforward to deal with. They lived in their own house in a small cul-de-sac right behind the shop, which was very convenient for the wife.

I was collecting my paraffin one day when I heard a dog yelping in the street outside, so, dressed in my uniform, I went outside to see what it was all about. A driver was parked close to the kerb and was examining a small dog lying in the gutter behind the car. I put my can down and took a close look at the dog; it seemed unconscious and had obviously been run over. Stray dogs were a regular sight in those days and often met their fate in this way; you would see whole packs of them following a bitch on heat and they frequently chose to perform in the middle of the road oblivious to the stopped traffic, often causing great consternation and throwing of buckets of water when they became locked!

I decided to call a vet, so I went back into the shop to use their telephone, but then I heard the car start up again and, through the shop window, I saw it reverse back over the dog. Before I could get outside the deed was done.

The driver said, "I couldn't leave it in pain so I have put it out of its misery!" I was 'shell-shocked' for a few seconds and before I could say another word, he had driven off.

Some weeks later, I was called to the little shop and as soon as I arrived, I could see the reason for my visit; the main front window, some 12 foot square, had been smashed right in the middle. A large stone lay inside the shop and the staff were busy clearing up the mess. It transpired that the damage had been done the previous evening although no one could pinpoint the exact time. Mrs Hancock was furious at the mess and even more at the cost that would be involved to replace the plate glass. I recorded the crime, obtained an estimate of the cost involved and took a statement from Mrs Hancock.

Bearing in mind who her husband was and that he would certainly hear all the details, I set off to make thorough enquiries at nearby houses. "I am making enquiries about the damage to the window at the hardware shop along the road. Did you see or hear anything which might help me find the person responsible?" I repeated this to everyone within a 200 yard circle around the shop. It seemed that not one had heard or seen anything and I was left with my crime completely unsolved.

Later that day I rang the station at Kidsgrove to be answered by none other than Sergeant Hancock himself. "A bit of a nasty incident at the shop last night. How are your enquiries going?" he said. I had to admit that so far I had drawn a blank with my house to house enquiries but I said I would be asking around the local youths to see if they could throw any light on the matter. Later, I spent at least two hours seeking out the local 'yobs' in a desperate attempt to trace anyone who could help.

If only I could find a suspect; it would be easy to pin him down by sending his clothes for forensic examination. Later in my career, I found a tramp lying in a haystack near to a derelict house which had been set on fire. Although I could smell smoke on his clothing he had been too drunk to remember what had happened. He had not been seen in the house but it seemed obvious that he had smashed a window to gain entry and then to get warm, had lit a fire in the middle of an upstairs bedroom. Anyone with any sense would have realised that a wooden floor was not the place to light a fire, but in his drunken state he had been oblivious to danger. When the fire took hold, he had made his way downstairs and wandered to the hayrick some 100 yards away to sleep it off. I arrested him and we obtained a solicitor to argue his case. He could remember nothing of the incident so, as a last resort, I sent his thick coat off for examination together with the broken pieces of glass from the window. The report came back with conclusive evidence that he was only a few feet from the window of the house when the glass was broken - the scientists compared minute fragments of the glass in his coat and could say that it was from the same window in the house. When, for instance, a stone is thrown at a window, the minute particles of glass shower out in all directions for great distances; the main pieces obviously fall to the ground nearby but some will enter the culprit's clothing. When presented with this evidence, the tramp pleaded guilty to arson, following advice from his lawyer.

I was to have no such luck with this window and as it was the only outstanding crime in the village at the time, I was more than anxious to clear it up. The problem is that, as time passes, the trail gets colder and colder; but I never gave up with the case and one very good reason was the constant reminders from

Sergeant Hancock and his wife! They maintained an interest in the matter for a number of weeks before they gradually seemed to forget about it by which time I was certainly relieved not to be constantly reminded of my inability to solve such a simple matter. But in the back of my mind, it remained the most important enquiry I had on the files. Days turned into weeks and weeks into months. The window had long since been replaced and the knowing smile from Mrs Hancock said it all - I was forgiven, providing I kept a better watch on the shop from now onwards!

But as I said; I had not given up on the enquiry and at every opportunity I would ask the local children what they could remember. Then one evening, I was on patrol on the estate when I saw a group of 12 year olds playing football on the half moon grassed area in front of their homes. They all suddenly came my way and despite my inability to play football, I kicked it back to them, accidentally scoring a goal.

My, were they impressed by the local bobby joining in their game - normally the police just shouted at them. I used this sudden moment of favour to ask them again, "About six months ago the window was broken in the shop down the road. Can any of you remember what happened?" It was a shot in the dark and a question I had already asked time and time again. I half expected them to say something like, "you always ask us that Mister," but this time the response was not what I was expecting. One of the lads blurted out.

"I know who broke it but he doesn't live round here now!" This was music to my ears; at last someone knew something about it. Could my luck run to finding out a name, I thought, as I had another kick at the ball.

"He lives in Tunstall now. It was the last day he lived here when he broke it."

After this it was easy; I obtained the boy's name after promising not to tell anyone who had given me the information. I had built up a certain trust with people in the village by dealing fairly but firmly with wrong-doers and now it was paying off. Perhaps if his friend had still lived in the village, the boy would have been unwilling to 'grass' on his mate, but time had caused any allegiance to fade.

I went back to the station and began checking both the phone book and the electoral register. It was a long shot, but the village boy had been to the offender's house once and had given me a fair idea of its location. I knew I needed to plan my next move carefully; it is always difficult obtaining a confession even when you have a witness to the incident but when you are trying to hide the identity of an informant, it makes the job even harder. I established an address in Tunstall and had a good idea where the house was. My approach would now be of the utmost importance; one wrong move or a word out of place and I would blow the gaff on all my hard work.

In those days, most children had a healthy respect for their parents with only the most unruly choosing to lie to them. I had already deduced that mothers tend to seek the truth deeper and are more likely to be on the side of law and order. Later in my career, I found that attitudes changed and I was often met with the pronouncement, "You prove he did it or get out!" Fortunately, this was not the case in the mid 1960s and also, I was not required to have a social worker or solicitor in on the act. It would be better to see the boy with only one parent present, and surprise was on my side; the time lapse would have lulled him into a false sense of security and he would be confident that his secret was safe for the rest of his days. I did wonder whether his old mates might warn him of my enquiries - this caused me to act as quickly as possible.

I did not want his father at home when I called, so I set off to Tunstall at 3.30pm the following day which would give me time to find the house and go for the kill by 4pm. I had no written evidence of course, or indeed any proof that he was responsible for the broken window, therefore, if he decided to plead ignorant of the offence, I was in great difficulties. I needed to play on his weaknesses - the shock of my arrival; the fact that I knew he left Talke Pits on the day after the window was broken and if necessary, I would have to pretend that I was in a position to produce a witness to the crime - this last device only be used in an emergency. I approached the door carrying a buff folder which looked as if it contained important evidence - in reality only the crime complaint sheet, and I put on an air of confidence. By all appearances, they had gone up in the world rather; the house was spick and span, the brass letter box was polished and the net curtains were bright white with neat little pleats.

The door was opened by the boy, still in his school uniform. He just looked at me, obviously too frightened to utter a word. His mother came down the stairs and shouted.

"Who is it, Michael?" He stood motionless and said nothing so I shouted back for him.

"I am a policeman; can I have a word with you please, madam?" His mother came straight to the door and invited me in.

"Yes, come in. What is the problem officer?" she asked. We went into the front room where Michael had spread his school books on the floor ready to do his homework.

"I am sorry to have to come unannounced but I am from the police station at Talke Pits." The boy's face was a picture as I said this and I knew that he realised his secret was out.

"I think you should tell us what went on the day before you left the village. I know what happened and you know, but your mother does not. You tell her Michael," I said, staring at him. His mother looked very worried but sat back and said,

"Right, Michael; I want to know what the policemen has come about. What on earth have you been up to?"

This was just what I needed, backing from a concerned parent. Statements such as this from parents are actually frowned upon now especially in the presence of someone in authority like me. Any answer under 'duress' would not be allowed in evidence but my hands were fortunately not tied by such nonsense then! Michael started to mutter some words.

"Is it about the window?" This was music to my ears again. His mother wanted to know more.

"What window are you talking about, Michael?"

Michael held his head down in shame and looked at the carpet as the story unravelled. He had been out for a celebration on the night and had been throwing stones. One large one went straight through the store window and everyone ran home. The story was brief and to the point! I needed a statement and I told her that, as many months had passed and the boy was under 14 years of age, there was little more to be done. The details would be forwarded to the insurance company but it was doubtful if they would follow it up. A short statement was obtained which she signed and I left, apologising for causing a disturbance to her household. I have no doubt that when Michael's father returned from work, the feathers would fly, but it was all in the boy's own interest, of that I was completely certain. After all he no longer needed to keep his secret from the outside world and what a weight off his shoulders that would be!

I climbed back into my old Ford Popular and drove directly to Kidsgrove. Sergeant Hancock would still be on duty and I couldn't wait to see his reaction to my news. All of those little comments would be erased now. I had a grin on my face like a Cheshire cat as I pulled up outside the station, and before going in, I sat and filled out the crime complaint result sheet thus:

PERSONS RESPONSIBLE:
Michael ....; Age 12 years
STATEMENT OF ADMISSION: - YES

I tried to look casual as I approached the sergeant at his desk.

"Unusual for you to call at this time, Trevor," he said.

"Yes Sarge; I have just been to Tunstall to sort out that broken window of yours."

"You don't mean the shop where my wife works; I thought we had filed that one away a long time ago," he replied.

I maintained a straight face and said casually, "Yes, it was about six months ago, I think. I have continued my enquiries and this afternoon I found the person responsible. Perhaps you would tell you wife for me?"

I tossed the statement sheet and the completed crime complaint on his desk and said, "I think everything is clear from the statement. He is only 12 years old so there will bc no court proceedings. I'm sorry it took so long but that's how things go sometimes, Sarge!"

His face changed as he read the statement and he grinned from ear to ear. No further words were needed between us.

His wife came out of the shop to speak to me as I walked past the next day. My efforts had clearly not gone unappreciated – I could just imagine the conversation between them when they realised that I had solved their unsolvable crime after all this time.

ONE PINT PLEASE

Allow me to take you back to the days when the Coop corner shop would take your order on a Friday night and deliver it in a cardboard box on Saturday at no extra charge; when the shopkeeper referred to you as 'Madam' and when you collected your 'divi' at the end of eaeh financial year - it was quite something to receive two shillings and sixpence in the pound back, just for being a loyal customer. Supermarkets did not sell milk because every household used the early morning delivery service provided by dozens of operators. People made good businesses out of starting up milk rounds, as long as their product was of good quality and their price were fair. The Coop started its milk rounds in Stafford with a horse and cart loaded with milk churns, dispensing the milk into your own jug from the cart. Sometimes it would still be warm if the roundsman collected his own supply from the farm.

We had moved on from this by the mid 1960s and all milk was in bottles, having been processed before delivery. Competition between milkmen was fierce with great deals available for anyone wishing to change their supplier; you could opt for a fortnight's free milk as a thank you for changing over, or, if it was near Christmas, you might be offered a free turkey. If your milkman changed his route and the fresh milk started to arrive at 11am when you really needed it at 8am, then it was just the excuse you needed to finish with him and to start with someone else! Moving house was watched with 'eagle eyes' by every milkman for miles around; you had hardly put the first stick of furniture through the front door before milkmen were lining up to tell you what you could expect from them if you placed an order - notes pushed through the door were not seen as user friendly, so each milkman came in person to persuade you!

This situation was the background to an incident which caused me a number of sleepless nights - most unusual for me! The initial report was made to the CID at Kidsgrove. It was one of those minor complaints of theft which the CID in their wisdom chose to pass on to me; it had the immediate hallmarks of being insoluble and even if the culprit was caught, no kudos was likely to accrue.

I called in at the station to collect my routine bundle of paperwork, when Ernie asked if he could have a word with me. He was holding a scribbled message on a pad, which he handed to me with a slight snigger. "Can you call round at this one on your travels; the woman thinks her milk is being stolen from the step. I haven't recorded it at this stage because she seems a bit vague about what's going on. If you need any help, just give me a ring."

I took the note and saw that it was an address in Talke Pits on a new housing estate adjoining the council houses. The taking of a bottle of milk was one of those annoying offences in the same category as scrumping or taking a newspaper from a letterbox - of very low importance to the CID but of great concern to the victim - and indeed to me - I saw these petty crimes as being of equal importance to the burglary which netted antique jewelry. Ernie went back into his office, feeling safe in the knowledge that this incident would keep me out of mischief for weeks ahead! I could overhear the laughter as he explained to the detective sergeant how another major crime was about to be unravelled by the 'big hat brigade'!

That evening I set out on patrol with the scribbled message in my hand and walked the mile or so to the complainant's home. I wondered how the lady could be vague about the theft of milk from her doorstep; after all, it has either been stolen or it has not; it was as simple as that as far as I was concerned. I rounded the corner and started looking for the number of the house, using my torch to illuminate the various porchways. Some owners had decided that instead of a house number they would use a name; others seemed to feel that investing in numbers one inch tall made of solid brass would impress everyone. They might look fancy but for the postman, doctor, fire brigade or police, they were of less use than ornament. Perhaps the dustbins outside the council houses just down the road, with great daubs of white paint on them showing their house numbers, were not so ugly after all! At least they helped unfortunate people like me to find the address.

My torch beam eventually alighted on the right house, although it was necessary for me to venture half way up the front path to do so, since the main door was on the side of the house! It was a neat little semi-detached with a lawn at the front and as it was only a few years old, there was a garage at the back. The drive was shared until a point at the start of the building line where it widened into two drives with a small privet hedge in the middle; no doubt this hedge gave some privacy, especially as the two back doors faced each other. I rang the door bell and waited, gazing around in order to collect information.

My detective sergeant had given me the advice of always using the back door entrance to a house; the kitchen and hall were much more likely to show you things of interest than being led straight into the front room via the front hallway. The same detective sergeant also had a nasty habit of not knocking at doors, but just pushing them in with his shoulder, catching the unwary by surprise; when the need for a warrant was ever suggested, he would mutter, "I knew there was something I'd forgotten; never mind, it's too late now for that!"

The door was opened by a woman in her mid 30's, smartly dressed and with several young children following her every move.

"Hello, I have come about the problem you've been having with the milk," I said.

"Oh yes, officer; come in. I rang the station yesterday and was expecting someone to call."

The home was very clean and apart from a liberal scattering of childrens' toys, was very orderly and tidy. First impressions are most important and certainly would add credibility to any claim she made.

"Would you like a cup of tea, officer?" she said, heading for the kitchen. I never refuse such an offer and replied, "Yes, one sugar please, with milk," I hoped that this of all days was not one chosen by the milk thief to strike!

She returned a few minutes later with the tea on a tray complete with biscuits. I started to try and establish what had been going on regarding the milk.

"Since we moved in here some two years ago, the milk has been delivered to the door by the Polish milkman. On most days we have two pints but sometimes we have three. I leave the milk basket out and turn the little dial around so that he knows how many I want," she said.

I asked, "Do you pay for it weekly or leave the money out each day?" I was aware that only the Coop had a system of small checks which were bought at the Coop shops and left out on the step.

"No, he calls every Friday for the money which is when I found out that something was wrong. It doesn't happen every week and at first I was unsure if it was just a mistake by the milkman or me. He was charging me for more bottles than I had had. At first he said he was sorry and charged me for what I said I had had, but now he says he has kept an accurate record and some weeks I have had to pay for more than we have used. I know it sounds peculiar but both of us are sure we are right," she continued.

I said, "It is a little confusing; are you saying that you think your milkman is trying to cheat you into paying for more milk than he delivers?"

"Oh no, I don't think he's that kind of person. He has been fine for almost two years now; very reliable and friendly. He seems as sorry as we are and it was him who told me to report it to the police. I don't think he would do that if he was trying to cheat us, do you?" she said. It certainly did not seem plausible for him to be cheating his customers and then telling them to call the police.

"Have you kept a record of how many bottles you have asked for each day?" I enquired.

"Yes, I have and so has the milkman. On Tuesday, I ordered three bottles and made a note of it. Then when I went to get it, there were only two. I rang him straight away and he told me that he definitely left three bottles on the doorstep. We have checked it several times before I called you - you are the last resort! We don't want to waste your time but I need to know what's going on. It's very worrying; if someone is stealing the milk, they might start stealing something else next!"

I finished my tea and told her that I would visit the milkman at his dairy tomorrow. Just before I left, I asked, "By the way, what time does he deliver the milk and when do you bring it in."

She replied, "He comes very early, while we're still asleep and we get up at eight. I go straight to the milk now to see how many bottles are there."

"Leave it with me; I will get to the bottom of it for you, whatever it takes," I promised.

A meeting with the milkman was arranged by telephone and the following day I left the village to see him at the dairy. He was waiting there ready for me and shook hands with me. He still retained a thick Polish accent although his English was good. He told me that he came to England at the start of the War and had fought for us then until the War ended when he came back to England and started the milk round. He had now expanded to two delivery trucks carrying eggs, potatoes and sometimes even vegetables. He seemed in all respects an upstanding citizen with a high regard for the laws of his new country. His explanation of events followed exactly that of his lady customer and he was sure that he had delivered the correct amount each day; somehow they must be being spirited away! He had just one thing to add to the story, making matters even more complicated. On odd days when the family only ordered two pints, sometimes both would go missing and the lady would rise to find that the two empty bottles were still in the milk basket from the night before! So was it possible that the thief drank the milk and then left the empties?

No amount of questioning was going to resolve the matter and I now realised why the CID had presented me with the problem. The milkman seemed to be almost eliminated from suspicion. As I left, I remembered one important last question,

"By the way; what time do you deliver to the house," I asked, somewhat unprepared for the reply.

"Oh, it's one of my first streets; I get up at 3 o'clock and deliver to her house not later than 4o'clock," he said.

That was just what I didn't want to hear. My observations would mean waking at 3.30am at the latest to be in position for the action. It was mid-winter and it was cold enough walking around the village in the daytime but standing still in the middle of the night would be almost unbearable. Did he really say 4am? I crossed being a milkman off my list of possible careers without further hesitation! Staying up from 10pm to 6am was almost a pleasure when compared with rising at 3am every day!

I did not tell him what action I would be taking and I also thought about keeping it from the lady herself. But any observations would mean me creeping around her home in the middle of the night and I wanted to avoid the embarrassment of disturbing the family. One false move might provoke a 999 call with the traffic car finding the culprit to be only me hiding behind a hedge! No, I would have to tell the family so I went back to the house and explained that when it was my duty days, I would start watching just before 4am and would probably still be in their garden when they rose and went to get the milk. The woman looked at me in disbelief. I could imagine what was going on in her mind. She was not thinking my actions were a sign of dedication more a sign of some kind of premature senile dementia!

Duties were adjusted with Kidsgrove to allow me to start early, with the usual wisecracks such as, "She must be a good-looker to get you out of bed that early; or even less subtle ones like, "How are you going to get rid of the husband for a few days?" But I took it all with a pinch of salt and was more determined than ever to get to the bottom of it.

The alarm clock was set for 3.30am and I went to bed early. The pattern of thefts showed that things could be normal for a couple of weeks and then happen on two days running. It only seemed like seconds before the alarm clock went off; my eyes would not open at first, until the thought of catching the villain red-handed got me going. I put on as many layers of clothes as I could fit beneath my great coat and set off towards the estate, closing the front door quietly behind me so as not to disturb my sleeping family. The ground was covered with a thick layer of frost, sticking to the soles of my shoes and falling off in great chunks. As I looked back, my steps stood out clearly in the glow of the street lights; this would help me, I thought, to follow anyone who had the audacity to run off when I confronted them.

The cold soon got to my finger tips through my standard issue leather gloves; my ears tingled and my nose started to run. It would have been so easy for me at that moment, just to mark it off as an unsolved crime, or to put in a general complaint form requiring the night patrol to pay visits; but no, this was my crime and solve it I would! When I arrived, I was mindful of my tracks in the thick frost and I walked up the drive on the kerbstones to make them less obvious.

Despite arriving at 4am, the Polish milkman had beaten me to it; there in the container were three full bottles, just as requested on the dial. Now it was a matter of patience but if you have ever tried to stand in one place for about four hours in the middle of the night, you will know what real boredom is! For well over two hours, hardly a thing moved. The houses looked so warm and cosy inside whilst outside the frost was forming on my great coat.

I found a vantage point at the side of the next door's garage from where I could watch the drive and the milk bottles. I moved about a little, just as much as I dared and took the comfort of the occasional cigarette - at least it gave me something to do; I had recently been at the sharp end of a price rise in a packet of cigarettes and had invested in a roll-your-own machine. It was taking some getting used to; a packet of papers, a pouch of rolling tobacco and the machine itself. You needed to be a juggler to get the whole lot out of your pockets together and then produce something even resembling a cigarette! Most of the time they came out like a very thin fuse and when you lit them, they burnt just like one, giving me about three puffs before my fingers got burnt.

By 6am I was really cold, thirsty and, by now, getting hungry. One lesson was being learnt quickly; always take a flask of something warm and a bar of chocolate at least! The sound of clinking milk bottles could be heard in the distance, being carried on the night air and paper boys were in evidence now, pushing their newspapers through the letterboxes and they were soon followed by the postman. The time ticked by agonisingly towards

8am. The house lights finally came on at 7.15am and I knew my ordeal was nearly over. But the milk was still in its place when the lady opened the back door to take it in. "Hello," I said in a quiet voice, trying my best not to startle her.

"I didn't realise you would be starting so soon," she said, followed by the welcome offer of a drink of hot tea. She was somewhat alarmed that my coat was encrusted with fresh frost and thanked me profusely for trying to catch the culprit. The warmth of the house soon made my ears and face tingle before they went a bright red. The husband came down stairs and gazed at me in amazement.

"I'm so sorry that you have had to keep watch for so long officer. What time did you start?"

I don't think he really believed me when I told him! And he believed me even less when I said that I would do exactly the same until I caught the thief. I left for home after drinking my tea and spent the best part of the morning thawing out in front of the fire; which may not be the best way to return the body temperature to normal, but felt like heaven!

Word had gone around the station about my exploits although no one dared to say anything to me. The general opinion was that if I was mad enough to get up at that time over a bottle of milk, what lengths would I go to to deal with anyone who criticised me for it?

The following night the clock was set again and the procedure repeated. The frost had gone but the boredom was just as bad. The delivery was a little later this morning and I watched as the milkman placed the bottles in the container and then crept out and checked that they tallied with the requested number. Soon, as the days went by, I found myself taking an interest in the times each family got up and in all their little routines. Some had coal fires with ashes to empty and sticks to chop for kindling; dustbin lids were discarded and ashes thrown into the metal bins making clouds of dust. Some had no curtains in the bathroom, seeming to believe that the frosted glass afforded sufficient privacy - it was quite entertaining watching members of one family trooping in and out of the bathroom wearing little more than a pair of sagging underpants; I got very good at identifying each by their silhouettes and at times I was so pre-occupied, that I had to quickly check the number of full milk bottles again, in case the thief had visited without me seeing him.

The days drifted on without success but what was most annoying was the fact that sometimes the milk went missing when it was my day off! I tried to dismiss this as just bad timing, however I was beginning to think in the back of my mind that someone could be watching me! The weather suddenly worsened with snow flurries blowing from the north. I was in my third week of observations now and to be quite honest, even I was about to give up. No one could say I had not given it my best shot! But by now I was actually used to getting out of bed at an unearthly hour and I had found a little world to amuse myself. The snow had been welcomed by the estate children and snowmen had appeared in abundance.

The next door's garden had become covered with sledges and an old kitchen chair - I assumed the children had used it to stand on when fitting the snowman's head and scarf. Anyway, the chair was put to good use and gave me a well earned rest! What amused me after, was that my large boot prints in the fresh snow had not seemed to arouse the neighbours' curiosity in the slightest. I can't guess who they thought was wandering in and out of their garden in the dead of night; no wonder the complainant could never find the culprit when her next door neighbours never even noticed or mentioned great big foot prints all over their garden!

I had finally decided to call it a day at the end of the next week and told the lady of my decision. She was very understanding and agreed that I had done my best. But the following morning my luck was about to change. I arrived before a single bottle had been delivered and was ready waiting in the drive to greet the Polish milkman.

We walked down the drive quietly together, discussing the past weeks' events - or the lack of them. Then I asked him straight out, "Tell me, who you think is doing it?"

Without the slightest hesitation, he said, "It's another

milkman, I reckon; someone's trying to get my customers off me and trying to make me look unreliable. Why else would the empty bottles be there when I have delivered full ones."

I asked him which one, then, did he think was doing it and he was about to reply when we both heard the sound of bottles clinking.

He said, "I think it's this one coming now. I'll go and you can hide again, and he ran back to his float and moved further down the street while I went back into hiding.

Within a few minutes, I saw the other float draw up at the end of the drive and the delivery man got out carrying a hand crate with six bottles in it and scurried up the drive. Behind the privet hedge, I could hear the sound of bottles being placed on the ground but then I knew that the Polish milkman did not deliver to next door. Then, all of a sudden, he burst through the hedge between the houses and made for the bottles. The hedge sprang back into shape immediately behind him. I watched as he approached the newly delivered milk, placed his crate on the floor and put two of the full bottles into it, exchanging them for two empty bottles, no doubt just collected from next door. If I had not seen it with my own eyes, I would not have believed it.

The smooth operator was off down the drive in a flash, heading for his float. I had been taken a little by surprise after all my waiting and by the time I was off my seat and in full chase he was almost in his cab. He still had his back to me and I clasped his right shoulder taking a firm grip.

"Right, Robin Hood; the game's up!" I said, pulling him round to face me. Where I conjured up these words from, I don't know, but that is exactly what I said.

"You are under arrest for stealing milk; you do not have to say anything unless you wish to do so, etc, etc."

His reply was a gem. "I did it out of habit; I'm sorry; it won't happen again!"

I said, "You will have to be careful what you are saying. It sounds to me as if you are admitting that you have done this before."

To say he looked petrified would be an understatement. He stuttered out excuses, each one worse than the one before. I had surely caught my man and now he would go before the magistrates! But despite all my planning, I had not thought what I would do if I caught someone, least of all what to do with a milk float loaded with milk. But resourceful to the end, I decided to offer him this option:

"There are two ways of getting to Kidsgrove; the first is that we lock the float up and together we walk the six miles from here or the second is, we go down in the float together. You decide. I've got all day so it makes little difference to me."

He decided on what was of course my preferred option and the two of us sat side by side in his electric float and sped off into the sunrise at about 5 miles an hour, the crates rattling gently as we bounced over bumps in the road. I sat there like a triumphant King of Persia, thinking to myself how not only had I satisfied my lady complainant and her honest milkman, but also added to my list yet another prisoner! He might not be Jack the Ripper but in my mind he was equally as important.

The journey was uneventful, taking about an hour. Motorists stared a little as they crept past in their cars and pedestrians were puzzled by my new form of police transport. I just hoped they would be thinking to themselves, how other wrongdoers would meet with the same fate as my prisoner.

At one point, we were stopped at traffic lights and he said, "Could I just drop a couple of bottles at that house on the corner?" I stared back at him and said, "You're a prisoner; don't ask such silly questions."

When we arrived at the station, a number of staff came out to greet us including the CID. We got out of the float and I clamped the handcuffs on the milkman, not for any other reason I suppose than to illustrate my success!

"Sergeant, I have arrested this man for stealing milk. I watched him take two bottles from a doorstep and walk off down the drive," I said, in a voice that could be heard all over the station. I sat down to write out a statement and was joined by an inquisitive Ernie.

"You have caught a milkman stealing milk!? That certainly is one for the book," he said with a smile.

"Yes; it was from that woman's house you asked me to check on; the one who was so confused about her milk disappearing," I said in a jaunty manner. "You just keep sending me these bits of information Ernie; I like following them up."

It transpired that the milkman was indeed trying to gain

customers from the other milkmen by making them look unreliable. He had been doing it at various houses on his round. The Court was impressed by my determination and imposed a large fine on him. I can only assume that the Polish milkman was also pleased - I did not see him again - I needed my beauty sleep too much: But I could only think it was he who left a large fresh turkey on my front doorstep a few days after the court case!

ARMED AND HOSTILE

Now that I come to put this story down on paper, it hardly seems conceivable that this story is true; but I can assure you it is. At the age of nineteen I was well used to operating on my own and, anyway, no amount of radios could help a lone constable at 2am on a Monday morning. Despite a population of some 10,000 inhabitants, all that stood between the public and our criminal fraternity at that time of the week was one constable, often me. It was great to finish a series of night shifts at the earlier time of 2am; which is what the Sergeant and his merry band of senior constables did on Sundays. Their duty would start at 6pm, four hours earlier than usual and end at 2am, which enabled them to rise afresh at 9am on Monday morning to start their three rest days off.

It was my role, then, to hold the fort and to remain for the four hours between 2am and 6am and answer any telephone calls, which to be fair were few and far between. This fact, no doubt eased the conscience of those chosen for an early finish but it did not reduce the anxiety felt whenever the telephone did ring. A direct telephone line connected Kidsgrove to the main divisional station at Newcastle and these were the instructions I was given should a call require me to leave the station: 'Ring Newcastle and tell them where you are going and why; a car will be sent to look for you if you don't ring back when the job is finished, so don't forget to tell them when you return. When you go out, lock the station and put the key on the ledge above the door.'

"We will see you on Thursday," the Sergeant would say, as he left for his warm bed!

This kind of policing certainly sharpened your senses and it prepared me for the sort of back-up I would get at my next posting. It was a market town in the centre of the county, provided with two Panda cars and two vans for use in the surrounding rural areas. Most people would describe it as a sleepy market town which only came to life every Wednesday when the cattle market was in full swing.

My enthusiasm could not have been exceeded as I launched myself onto the unsuspecting public. Farmers, by and large, conform with most laws and it is usually from a blend of ignorance and stubbornness that they break them. Overtime payments were the life blood of most young officers and therefore on Wednesdays, which were decreed as my rest days, I could be found working for the market auctioneers, ensuring that the centre of the market was kept free of traffic. We all know how easy it is to leave our vehicles on yellow lines with the intention of loading or unloading, only to be distracted. A three minute job suddenly expands to half an hour without any difficulty at all – and in the case of farmers, this would often grow to three quarters of an hour or more! My job was to see that everyone attending the market could drive in, park and unload and then leave for the car park. It sounds simple but when Farmer Giles has not seen Farmer Fred from the neighbouring farm for several weeks, a conversation soon strikes up. Smallholders with one pig to sell, would arrive and produce the lone animal from the boot of an old mud-spattered car – a nice lining of straw in the vehicle denoted an enhanced status, in that you were both a landowner and a rearer of stock – and think they owned the market!

For two weeks I ran myself ragged asking the auctioneer to announce over the tannoy that a Land-rover and trailer was blocking the entrance to the calf pens, or would the driver of a cattle truck please return to it as three other vehicles were blocked in. Even when warnings were given to the miscreant drivers, a loss of memory would seem to overcome them by the next market day; it was quite obvious that more stern action was required to deter those who chose to be illegally parked – and the modern day parking ticket had not been invented then!

Farmers meeting together are extremely trusting and I could not recall any reports of items being stolen from the market. This flaw, I decided, was about to be exploited by me in an effort to encourage users of the short-stay parking arrangements to use it for just that! Sure enough, within minutes of starting my duty, a Land-Rover and trailer were parked near to the pig section. There were no animals in it and I allowed the driver ten minutes to return and remove it to the car park. As expected, the vehicle did not move and a long queue of assorted vehicles soon built up at the market entrance. This was my opportunity to test my new system. I entered the insecure vehicle and sat behind the wheel, placing my helmet on the passenger seat, or more precisely on top of the assorted debris which covered the seat. Nothing had prepared me for the state of a farmers vehicle and the stench of pig manure was truly awful, but this had to be done! Every vehicle parked was always left with its ignition keys in place, to allow it to be moved by fellow farmers if necessary; no doubt this practice had grown up over the years and while I could have taken advantage of this and moved the vehicle to the car park myself, it would not have solved the problem for me in the future.

I drove the Land-Rover very carefully making sure that the trailer did not 'cut corners' and collide with pedestrians or other vehicles. At last, I was out of the private market area, heading for the nearby housing estate where I selected a quiet road and neatly parked the offending vehicle. My next move was the icing on the cake and it made me chuckle to myself all the way back to the station. Having locked the vehicle, I conveyed the keys to the police station where they were entered in the miscellaneous property book.

When I returned to the market some 20 minutes later, it was not long before a worried farmer made his way towards me.

"Have you seen a Land-Rover and trailer? It was parked here while I unloaded," said the farmer with obvious concern.

"Yes, I have removed one from the market and parked it in one of the side streets because it was blocking the loading bay. The keys can be collected from the police station - the station officer will give you its exact location," I replied.

The look of amazement was well worth the effort I had put into the venture. After about half a dozen vehicles had been on the receiving end of this little manoeuvre word had quickly spread; whenever I was on market duty, the whisper soon went round making my duty much less stressful!

During my time in the town, my colleagues, of course, always rallied to give me assistance on the very rare occasions that matters got out of hand! One seemingly quiet Tuesday, I started duty at 2pm and set to washing my Austin 1100 Panda car before leaving the station to patrol my half of the town. The main street carried a large volume of mixed traffic but due to its narrowness, few problems were usually experienced. However, this day, outside the town picture house, for some unexplained reason, two cars had managed to hit one another head on and my presence was requested.

On arrival at the accident, I put out the SLOW signs on both approaches and went to the assistance of the occupants who had fortunately received relatively minor injuries. The first aid kit carried in the Panda was crammed full of arm slings and assorted bandages suitable for stemming the flow of blood from a missing limb, but no plasters for use in such an incident! All the bandages were in numbered boxes which meant nothing to the unfortunate would be first aider, but no doubt a great deal to an expert at the bandage packing factory; it was rather like opening Christmas presents without the advantage of feel and size since the boxes were all the same. A cut finger could result in a battlefield dressing being applied, consisting of a huge gauze pad and several feet of bandage to secure it!

By the time the sergeant arrived with a special constable, I was well into my stride, having dealt with the minor injuries and ordered suitable breakdown trucks for the crumpled cars. The sergeant was somewhat short in stature and came complete with the bushy moustache which was the norm for officers who had seen active service in the War. He was a friendly enough type but one of his peculiarities was to drive his police car with his face close to the windscreen and to keep checking that the handbrake was off. This habit made passengers feel extremely insecure as it was repeated every few miles; his left hand leaving the steering wheel, reaching for the handbrake lever and giving it a tug up before releasing it again. Perhaps, on reflection, I was the only one to notice it and anyway, who was I to criticise an ex-soldier who had no doubt served his country well!

Dressed in reflective bibs, the three of us marked the

position of the vehicles involved by making a chalk mark at each corner, following which I started to draw a sketch plan while the other two measured the distance from fixed points such as lamp posts. It may not be fully appreciated that failure to perform this simple task can prove crucial if a plan is required at Court. I have often seen what appear to be brilliant sketch plans reduced to a farce when the defence points out that the positions of the vehicles could be anywhere along a 100 yard stretch of road.

For one such serious incident to happen in a day was relatively uncommon in this sleepy town, but this afternoon was to be different. Just as we were transferring the first measurements to the sketch plan, our radios crackled into life; the call was to the sergeant and by the tone of the operator's voice, it was an urgent message.

"Report of a man with a gun threatening people. His parents are waiting for a patrol to arrive, can you attend please?"

I listened but as I was dealing with this accident already, it never occurred to me that I might become involved in this second incident, especially as I had never been allowed near a gun whilst on duty. Our ex-soldier would be ideally suited to this kind of situation, I thought. The radio again splurted out a message.

"Further update: the man is now inside the house with a large gun and it seems that his parents are outside on the footpath with other residents."

The sergeant walked purposefully towards me and took hold of the clipboard on which I was writing the measurements of the accident.

"I will finish the sketch plan; you take the special constable and attend to this chap with a gun," he said, checking his pocket for a pen to write with. No wonder he had survived a world war, I thought, as I roared off in the direction of the incident!

"It sounds like a bad one," said the special constable as another radio message came through:

"It seems that the chap with the gun has had a skinful of beer," said the controller. We rounded the corner to see a large crowd of people on the footpath and others standing at their front gates looking towards number 34.

I stopped the car well short of the crowd, put my helmet

on, and walked slowly towards them. An agitated man came to me almost immediately and said;

"He's had a lot to drink officer and we had an argument and then he came into the front room with a gun and pointed it at us. We all ran out but he stayed in the house." Even I realised that any type of gun is dangerous but some are worse than others and with this in mind I tried to establish what kind it was.

"It's a big one with a long barrel," his father said.

"A shotgun?" I queried,

"Don't know really, it all happened so quickly," came the reply.

My next move will fill all modern day experts with horror, but I can assure you that at the time it seemed the most logical thing to do! I moved everyone back to a safe distance and told my controller that I was going to check inside the house. The father and special constable were taken to one side and told of my plan. Perhaps it was something I had seen in a film or a TV programme like the 'Sweeny', or perhaps it just entered my head out of the blue.

"We can't just wait for something to happen, we must go into the house. Whereabouts do you think he is?" I asked the father.

"He went upstairs, so I think he will still be up there," he replied.

"Right, I will go in first, through the front door and up the stairs. I want you to follow me," I said, pointing to the special constable. "And you follow him," I said, pointing to the father. "If anything happens to me, just grab the gun!"

It all seemed a good plan at the time, but how stupid it sounds in a modern day context; the 'SWAT' team would be summoned, together with trained negotiators and there would be a helicopter monitoring the position from above!

I walked past the assembled crowd and in total silence went towards the front door which was slightly ajar, the staircase just visible. I was aware of the two men behind me as I entered the house and quietly started to climb the stairs. You could have heard a pin drop as I reached the top and looked behind me for my back-up team - the two of them must have been in the same regiment as the sergeant - both had stopped outside the front door and were looking up the stairs! I admit I was as terrified as they were, but something made me keep calm and determined to go on and complete the job.

Having seen the result of firearms being fired close range at bodies, I knew that even my thick blue mackintosh was of no use against shotgun pellets, and if the gun was the type that fired bullets, it was quite likely to pass straight through my body. If things went badly, my actions would be seen as foolhardy - even stupid in the extreme - by those not inclined to speak kindly of the dead!

I stopped on the landing and saw several doors none of which were fully closed. I started with the door nearest to me and slowly pushed it open, trying not to make any sound; surprise had to be my main weapon in the absence of a bullet-proof vest and a semi-automatic gun! The open door revealed an empty bathroom and I was now very aware of the sound of my own breathing as I moved to the second door, which had to be a bedroom. The door opened with only a slight noise caused by the door brushing the carpet and it revealed a double bed, two large wardrobes and a dressing table, but no suspect!

For a few seconds, I thought about the possibility of the fugitive having run off out of the back door before I had entered and this made me feel a little easier as I pushed open the next bedroom door. This was a child's room with stuffed toys lying on the single bed and posters of pop stars on the walls. It was 'Sods Law'; when given the choice of four rooms, it is bound to be the very last one you open! I pushed open the last door even slower than the previous ones, with the thought in my mind that if confronted by the gunman, I would throw my body back behind the brick wall, leaving only my arm exposed. By the time the door had been pushed three quarters open, I saw the shape of a gun barrel lying on the floor. Should I run in and stand on it or try to grab hold of it? The door was now wide enough for me to enter the room and it revealed my fugitive lying flat out on the bed. He was clearly asleep! I picked up the gun from the floor and breathed a sigh of relief that no blood had been spilt, especially mine. Now was my moment of glory.

"Come on, get up!" I said in a loud voice, at the same time pulling at his white T-shirt. He looked at me through glazed eyes, unable to grasp what was happening.

"You're under arrest!" I said, followed by the usual, "You don't have to say anything unless you wish to do so, etc."

He rose slowly to his feet and I placed handcuffs on his wrists - a slow process as my handcuffs were not the snap-on variety now used but an ancient type with a large screw key which needed several complete turns before each wrist was secure. They were one size only which meant that if your wrist was larger than usual, they would trap a piece of skin as they clicked into place. Luckily this did not happen on this occasion and I took hold of his arm and led him down the stairs and out through the front door into the sunlight. Who would have thought that such a feeble looking chap in an old T-shirt and trousers hanging round his hips could have caused so much bother?

As I pushed him towards the throng of people on the footpath, I caught a glimpse of his father, looking rather sheepish and standing with the special constable. No one said a word as I forced a way through the crowd until I heard a voice boom out; "Well done, officer! What is he going to be charged with?"

I looked towards the man and instantly recognised the familiar white shirt and black tie, almost hidden beneath a civilian jacket. It was none other than the Divisional Superintendent who had no doubt been on call at the time the incident was reported. I was not surprised to see him dressed only partly in uniform - it avoided him being recognised as a police officer and getting involved in matters he chose to ignore. The hat with braided peak and the stick, medals and ribbons, were only worn at ceremonial occasions and for giving instructions to assembled officers before some major incident; they remained safely in the wardrobe on days like this!

"I will charge him with a breach of the peace and some firearms offences to start with, Sir," I replied, pushing the prisoner into the rear seat of the Panda car. At least he had come to the scene and congratulated me I thought; which did not happen very often.

The special constable sat in the rear as we drove back to the station, where I sat down to write a statement for the Court. Within a few minutes the controller put his head round the door and confirmed what I had suspected, "It's only an air rifle after all, lad; never mind, you weren't to know! Anyway, the sergeant has been on the radio; can you get back to the scene of the accident?"

I took the keys to the Panda and drove back. Surely he can't still be dealing with it I thought! When I arrived, the scene was clear of vehicles, apart from the sergeant standing next to his Panda car.

"I've done the sketch plan for you, lad, and taken a statement from one of the drivers. All you have to do now is fill in the document details and describe how the accident happened."

I was speechless as he handed me the clipboard with the accident report book, sketch plan and statement. Perhaps my idea of leading from the front is different to that of others, but I vowed that if ever I reached a position of authority in the force, my own experiences would prevent me making the same mistake.

THE END

POLICE

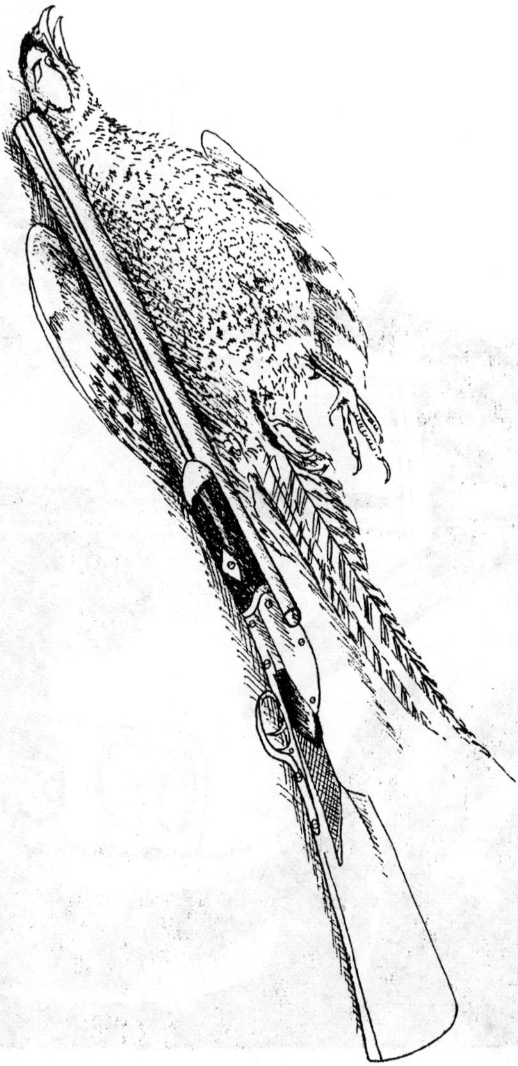